IN MEMORIAM

SO·THE·HEART·BE·RIGHT

Joanna Defrates

1945-2000

The First Hundred Years

EGYPTOLOGY
AT
UNIVERSITY COLLEGE LONDON
1892~1992

Cover illustration: Silhouette of Amelia Edwards. (From a copy of the marble bust in the National Portrait Gallery; drawn by Daphne Skinner.)

White marble bust of Amelia Edwards by Percival Ball, 1873. Bequeathed by the sitter to the National Portrait Gallery in 1892; now on permanent display in Bodelwyddan Castle, near St. Asaph, Clwyd, Wales. Height 63.5 cms. (MPG 929. Courtesy of the National Portrait Gallery.)

The First Hundred Years

EGYPTOLOGY
AT
UNIVERSITY COLLEGE LONDON

1892~1992

Rosalind M. Janssen

British Library Cataloguing-in-Publication Data.
A catalogue record for this book is available from the British Library.
Janssen, Rosalind
The First Hundred Years:
Egyptology at University College London 1892 - 1992

ISBN 0-902137-33-6

Designed and typeset by Ditas Rohl

Printed and bound in Great Britain by Laws and Stimson Associates,
31, Malden Way, New Malden, Surrey, KT3 6EB.

In Memory of

Violette Constance Lafleur
(1897 - 1965)

~ whose voluntary, single-handed, and
devoted wartime service rescued
Petrie's great collection from destruction ~
in gratitude

Contents

Preface

The Centenary of the Department of Egyptology at UCL is in many ways a very special event. The Edwards Chair, founded in 1892 through the generosity of the novelist and traveller Amelia Edwards, was the first chair in Egyptian archaeology to be established anywhere in the world, the earlier chairs in France and Germany being in the restricted field of Egyptian philology. What is more, this Centenary volume by Rosalind Janssen continues the tradition of UCL 'firsts' in that it is the first to be published anywhere which records the full history of a University Department of Egyptology.

Nor is that all. The first holder of the Edwards Chair was Sir William M. Flinders Petrie, a guiding hand in the establishment of the University of London's Institute of Archaeology which has, since 1986, become an integral part of UCL and an increasingly important and influential contributor to Ancient World Studies in the Faculty of Arts. It was to him that the then anonymous donor, Mrs. Mary Woodgate Wharrie, promised the £10,000 which he made over to Sir Mortimer Wheeler for an institute on condition that his own Palestinian collection should be housed and displayed in it.

Since the days when Flinders Petrie himself established the Predynastic chronology of Egypt, recorded in the artefacts now housed in UCL's Petrie Museum, the Department has, in the words of Negley Harte and John North's The World of UCL, 'stood at the centre of British archaeological effort in Egypt'.

The archival material in UCL records and in the Departmental and Museum archives, the manuscripts and rare books in the UCL Library, and the interviews on tape accumulated over the past five years, have all contributed to what I believe will prove, in its own way, to be another milestone in the history of Egyptian archaeology.

Dr. D. H. Roberts, C. B. E., F. R. S., F. Eng.
Provost of University College London

Foreword

The idea of writing an account of the vicissitudes of the Department of Egyptology at University College London germinated in 1985. In that year I presented a paper entitled 'The History of the Petrie Museum' at the Fourth International Congress of Egyptology, held in Munich. For this I utilized the Department's archival material, and was immediately struck by its scope and interest. I also began to talk to former members of staff and students about their time at UCL. From the spring of 1990 onwards, I was able to put these reminiscences on tape, in order to create a permanent record for future generations.

The Centenary of the Department in 1992 seemed to be an ideal and, at the same time, a unique opportunity to publish this information. I then began to expand the scope by using the College archives, housed both in the UCL Records Office and in the Library. It very soon became apparent that these sources were so rich that my initial plan for a fifty page booklet was a gross underestimate of their potential. So it grew from fifty through eighty pages, finally reaching the number of one hundred and five which the volume has today. At the same time, my interviews continued apace, and I was able to widen the circle of my informants by writing letters to those whom it was impossible to question personally because of distance. The response has been universal and the co-operation overwhelming. Although the edited reminiscences are designed to supplement the solid documentary material, this history would doubtless have made dull reading without them. Their accuracy has been checked whenever possible.

Finally, two points of explanation are needed. The account of the period from about 1960 until the present day has been deliberately curtailed, especially since the personal files of those still living are generally not yet accessible. An assessment of its achievements and the personalities involved must await a later, more detached biographer. The title of this Centenary volume is intended as a tribute to Margaret Murray who, at her own centenary, wrote her autobiography entitled *My First Hundred Years* (1963).

May the Department continue to flourish and reach in due course its second hundred years.

April, 1992

Acknowledgements

A long list of acknowledgements such as this reflects the great number of people on whom I have relied in this enterprise. The willingness and enthusiasm with which all have responded to my often repeated inquiries has never ceased to amaze me. Of each one I can only say that, but for his or her co-operation, something in this book would be missing.

For permission freely to utilize the archives under her care, I am indebted to Miss Elizabeth Gibson, the UCL Records and Administration Manager. The Supervisor, Miss Carol Bowen, has provided me with expert help throughout; her boundless enthusiasm and dogged persistence in tracking down the smallest detail, have been a constant source of wonder. Together with Miss Jaimé Imbeah, the Assistant, these three ladies of the UCL Records Office have been of immense practical assistance over many months. The happy atmosphere of the office will long be remembered. Indeed, it is true to say that without them this book could never have been written.

The College Librarian, Mr. F. J. Friend, allowed me to consult the Library Committee minutes and other documentation in his care. Facilities for this were kindly provided by his secretary, Mrs. Beatrice McDowell. For assistance in the Manuscripts and Rare Books section of the College Library, I am grateful to Miss Gillian Furlong.

It is equally certain that this book would never have been written had not Mr. E. M. Burgess, knowing my need, provided the Department with a most generous sum to purchase a cassette recorder which I could use for my interviews. This has proved absolutely indispensible in collecting the documentation. The following people were brave and magnanimous enough to allow me to record their reminiscences on tape: Mr. E. M. Burgess; Jean, Lady Carroll; Miss Margaret Drower (Mrs. Hackforth-Jones); Dr. I. E. S. Edwards; Mrs. Judith Hatton; Mrs. Diana Helbæk; Sir Laurence Kirwan; Dr. Violet MacDermot; Mr. J. Mellaart; Professor J. M. Plumley; Miss Sheila Puckle; Mrs. Julia Samson; the late Dr. M. Veronica Seton-Williams; Mr. E. P. Uphill.

Those who provided me with their memories in writing were: Dr. Kate Bosse-Griffiths; Professor H. Brunner; the late Professor R. Caminos; Mrs. Nonie Hamilton-Martin; Professor J. R. Harris; Dr. E. Iversen; Dr. G. Rudnitzky; Professor H. S. Smith; Mrs. Phyllis Spaull; Mrs. Lucia Turner. The considerable correspondence involved was most willingly typed by Mrs. Elizabeth Blyth, the Departmental Secretary. In addition, verbal communications were received from Mrs. Barbara Adams; Dr. D. M. Dixon; and Mr. H. M. Stewart.

The Photography and Illustration Centre of UCL deserves a special word of thanks. Mr. P. Harrison, Mr. S. P. Whalen, and Miss Mary Hinkley have copied and produced all the figures in this volume. For providing photographs or help with them, I am grateful to: Mrs. Betty Anson; Jean, Lady Carroll; Master Matthew Coy; Miss Margaret Drower; Mrs. Catherine Frankfort; Mr. J. Gill; Miss Elizabeth Miles at the Griffith Institute Oxford; the Hulton Deutsch Collection; the National Portrait Gallery; the Petrie Museum of Egyptian Archaeology, UCL; The Marquess of Northampton; Mr. L. Robinson-Smith; Miss Naomi Sargant (Lady McIntosh); The Times Newspapers Ltd.; Mrs. Lucia Turner; the UCL Records Office. To Miss Daphne Skinner's artistic skills we owe the silhouette of Amelia Edwards used on the front cover.

I am indebted to three enthusiastic research assistants: Mrs. Betty Anson; Dr. I. E. S. Edwards; and Professor J. J. Janssen. The latter spent many hours away from his own studies to assist me in the UCL Records Office and, in addition, read every word of the draft manuscript. The fact that he has endured a year's preoccupation with the history of a Department of Egyptology which is not his own, and is still ready to take an interest in it today, is sufficient tribute. Specific inquiries were answered by: Dr. M. Bierbrier; Mr. J. Lipley; Dr. J. Malek; Mr. R. F. Ovenell; Dr. W. J. Tait; and Dr. Helen Whitehouse.

Professor G. T. Martin authorized a generous grant from the Caton-Thompson Fund for the preparation and printing of this Centenary volume. He also read the draft manuscript, making many useful comments. Professor H. S. Smith did likewise, and provided me, from his vast knowledge, with valuable additions. He was a constant source of encouragement throughout.

Mrs. Ditas Rohl expertly typeset the manuscript, producing a camera-ready copy while bound to a strict deadline. The fact that she was willing to work entirely from my handwritten text deserves special commendation. Mr. D. Rohl was of considerable help, providing useful guidance and practical assistance from his wide experience of publishing. Last, but by no means least, Mr. N. Laws and Mr. J. Stimson, whose firm Laws and Stimson Associates printed this book, are to be thanked for their advice, efficiency, and reliability.

List of Illustrations

Chapter One

The Beginnings
1892~1893

On the 15th April 1892, Miss Amelia Ann Blanford Edwards, a distinguished Victorian popular novelist, died at the age of sixty-one (Frontispiece). Stress and overwork, brought on by her tireless campaign in the cause of Egyptian archaeology, had made her prey to a lung infection caught just six months earlier. In her will, drawn up a year before her death, she endowed a professorship in Egyptology at University College London (UCL), which would be the first chair at any British university for this subject. In this regard, we came years behind countries such as France, Italy, and Germany where Egyptology was already taught at universities.

But we should really look back nearly two decades for the starting point. It would never have happened had not Miss Edwards, by accident - to get out of the rain pursuing her during a stay in France - decided to take a trip up the Nile, in the winter of 1873-74. During this visit she was constantly appalled by the neglect and vandalism to which the ancient monuments were subjected. Her entertaining and informative travel story, *A Thousand Miles Up the Nile* (published in 1877), became an immediate bestseller, and would remain so through a revised edition until the end of the century. (It has recently been reprinted.)

From this time onward she devoted her life to Egyptology. Her contemporaries referred to her as the 'first woman Egyptologist', an apt description, for it was her dedication, remarkable powers of persuasion, and her popularization of the subject (particularly through her book *Pharaohs, Fellahs, and Explorers*) which helped to assure the future of British archaeology in Egypt, and to a large extent made it what it is today. She could perhaps best be called 'the godmother of Egyptology'.

It was she who was the real begetter of the idea of founding a society for the promotion and financing of excavations in Egypt. Thus in 1882 her brainchild the Egypt Exploration Fund (E.E.F.) was born, of which she became first joint Honorary Secretary. A year later this institution dispatched a certain William Matthew Flinders Petrie, a thirty year old Englishman, to the Nile Delta to excavate.

Petrie had first been to Egypt in 1880 in order to survey the Giza pyramids singlehanded. Before long he would make himself a name by his meticulous excavation methods, for he was a pioneer field archaeologist who recognized the value of small, seemingly insignificant objects such as pottery. When properly studied, they were, he argued, as important as most larger, more spectacular finds. This new methodology was to revolutionize the archaeology of the Nile Valley, and Petrie's basic principles are still adhered to by all modern Egyptologists (as well as by many excavators in other fields).

Miss Edwards was soon convinced that Petrie was the greatest contemporary Egyptian excavator. Over the following nine years he became her protégé and friend (Figure 1). The two of them found themselves much in sympathy over disturbing matters affecting the running of the Fund, and were to continue on terms of close friendship even when Petrie resigned from the E.E.F. in 1886 in disagreeable circumstances and started to excavate on his own account.

In her will, to which she had added a codicil three months before she died, Miss Edwards bequeathed nearly £5000, mostly in railway stock, to UCL. The income from it (amounting to £140 per annum), was to be applied to the founding of 'a Professorship in Egyptian Archaeology and Philology, includ-

1. *Amelia Edwards and her protégé, Flinders Petrie, c. 1890. (Courtesy of the Hulton Deutsch Collection; property of the Petrie Museum, UCL.)*

ing the deciphering and reading of hieroglyphs and other ancient Egyptian scripts and writings'. Also for use in connection with the professorship she bequeathed all her books, photographs, and other documents concerning Ancient Egypt, except her drawings and sketches; and all the Egyptian antiquities which she possessed. The latter comprised: 'my collection of ancient Egyptian jewellery; scarabs; amulets; statuettes of Deities in porcelain, bronze, and stone; funeral tables; sculptures; pottery; writings on linen and papyrus; and other miscellaneous monuments'.

The Council or governing body of University College was instructed to prepare rules and regulations with respect to the professorship in order to carry out to the best advantage her object in making the bequest. Her aim was: 'the teaching of Egyptology with a view to the wide extension of the knowledge of the history, antiquities, literature, philology, and art of Ancient Egypt'.

However, the bequest was also subject to five strict conditions. No person holding office at the British Museum was to be eligible for the professorship. The classes, scholarships and exhibitions were to be open to students of both sexes. The books and antiquities were to be housed in 'glazed bookcases and cases' and to be kept together in a room exclusively for this purpose (although additions to both could be made). The chair was to be called: 'The Edwards Professorship of Egyptian Archaeology and Philology'; and, finally, a plaque was to be placed over the door of the aforementioned room stating that 'the said books and antiquities and the said Professorship were the bequests of Amelia B. Edwards, with the dates of my birth and death'. As far as this final clause is concerned, present day visitors will notice that such a plaque is indeed positioned over the exit door of the Edwards library. We also have a copy of the bust of our foundress which was made from the original 1873 version (Frontispiece).

The College further received the copyright of Sir Erasmus Wilson's book *The Egypt of the Past*. This solid historical study had first been published in 1881. (It is of interest to note that this was the first work on Ancient

2

Egypt ever read by the great Egyptologist Sir Alan Gardiner, whom we shall meet again later on in our story.) The author, an eminent surgeon, had been Professor of Anatomy and Physiology at UCL. An Egyptophile, he was the first Treasurer and the first President of the E.E.F. as well as a munificent contributor. On his death in 1884 he had bequeathed the rights to this publication to his friend Miss Edwards. The second edition of 1887 had been revised and much enlarged by her, so that the idea behind her own bequest was that each subsequent edition should be revised by a competent Egyptologist, perhaps by the professor himself. The profits from sales would go to the holder of the chair in addition to his salary. In 1912 the matter came up in the Committee of Management of the College. Petrie (by then the Head of Department) stated that at that moment copies were still available and that it had been superseded 'by a work of himself on the same subject'! Since then, it seems never to have been discussed again.

This part of the will ends by stating that if the College failed to accept the bequest or at any time ceased to comply with the various particulars and conditions, it was to be offered to the University of Oxford under the same stipulations.

Her codicil of the 22nd January 1892, surprisingly enough, first reiterates that no official of the British Museum shall be eligible for the chair, but then adds the additional clause: 'Neither shall the first Professor occupying the Chair be a man above forty years of age'. It was further stated that if the College did not set apart a good and well-lighted room under the conditions specified in her will for her collection of Egyptian antiquities then she bequeathed this to the Ashmolean Museum, Oxford, under the same conditions. If they failed to fulfil the same, then it was to go to the Fitzwilliam Museum, Cambridge.

The reasoning behind some of Amelia Edwards' clauses require further elucidation. This active defender of women's rights had chosen University College London since this was the only academic institution at that time open for them to be admitted to degrees by examination. She had debarred any official of the British Museum from her professorship in order to prevent an application from E. A. Wallis Budge, Assistant Keeper in the Department of Egyptian and Assyrian Antiquities, since he had throughout been hostile to the E.E.F. The codicil requiring that the

first appointee be under forty years of age was to rule out other undesirables. Flinders Petrie was at the time of Miss Edwards' death rising thirty-nine. Clearly, she had been prepared for her imminent and premature demise.

Petrie is mentioned by name in the will, but in connection with certain annuities purchased in her name and held by her in trust for him. She refers to him as 'my friend William Matthew Flinders Petrie' and states that 'it is his wish that the said sum of annuities shall be added to the fund which I have appropriated for the purpose of founding the said Professorship'. She also appointed him to finish the labelling and cataloguing of her collection, for which he largely knew the exact provenance. He was to be paid £50 for his trouble. All this would seem to be an indirect pointer as to her feelings concerning the first incumbent.

Indeed, Amelia Edwards had seen to it that her wishes were more directly known to her executors, one of whom was her close friend and residuary legatee Miss Kate Bradbury (see Figure 4). The post would not only give Petrie the academic status he needed, but also a small fixed income, the security for his future work, together with a chance to train up students to follow in his footsteps.

Thus it was that in June 1892 the solicitors acting as Miss Edwards' executors, wrote to the Secretary of University College concerning the bequest. Their letter advises that the room to contain the property, comprising three hundred octavo volumes and the 'considerable' collection of antiquities, should consist of about 120 square feet of suitable glass cases on the walls and tables, at the least, 'while it is desirable that further space should be available for future additions'. As the books and antiquities were in their late client's house at Westbury-on-Trym, Bristol, which the executors were anxious now to dispose of, they requested the earliest possible decision from the College concerning the bequest.

Four days later, on the 2nd July, the College Council convened. The letter from the solicitors was read and it was resolved: 'That Miss Edwards' bequest be accepted, with the conditions named in the Will, and that the executors be informed that the Council will prepare as soon as possible, a room to contain the collection of Egyptian antiquities'.

At a further meeting on the 29th of the same month the Council resolved: 'That in consideration of Mr. Flinders Petrie's eminent qualifications as an Egyptologist and of the well-known wish of Miss Amelia Edwards that he should be the first occupant of the Chair which she has endowed, the Council dispense with advertisement of the Chair, and propose to appoint Mr. Petrie thereto; and that the Senate be requested to report to the Council before November 5th next their opinion on this appointment.'

Meanwhile, the candidate himself was being kept very busy during the late summer with the preparations for his annual exhibition to be held at 4, Oxford Mansion, Oxford Circus. For this month-long viewing he was expected to make his own showcases, arrange the objects, and write the accompanying catalogue. He had been in Egypt when Amelia Edwards died, digging at El-Amarna in what was one of his most spectacular seasons. The first modern excavations at this virgin site, capital of Akhenaten and Nefertiti, yielded beautiful sculptures and reliefs, as well as glazed tiles and inlays looking as fresh as the day when they had first been made in their accompanying pottery moulds. They still delight the eyes of visitors to the Petrie Museum.

The exhibition opened on the 19th September. Earlier in the month Petrie had been involved in the Ninth International Congress of Orientalists which met at UCL. He presented one of the first papers, which naturally revolved around his recent discoveries at El-Amarna, and was delivered to a packed hall and very favourably reported in the daily press. The following day he gave a second lecture, this time in the Geography section. A journal reported that he had been 'the man oftenest praised in the Congress', which doubtless helped to give his academic career a flying start.

On the 5th November the College Council met again and 'read a recommendation of the Senate in favour of the appointment of Mr. Petrie to the Edwards Chair of Egyptology'. A motion was then proposed and seconded with the result that it was resolved: 'That Mr. W. M. Flinders Petrie be appointed Edwards Professor of Egyptology'. The matter had been a foregone conclusion, for three days earlier the Secretary had written to Miss Bradbury telling her: 'You may take it for granted that he will be appointed to the Professorship'.

The Petrie Museum is fortunate enough to possess in its archives Petrie's formal letter accepting the Edwards Chair. Dated the 8th November, it is important enough to be extensively quoted:

I am much obliged to you [the Secretary] for your letter of yesterday, announcing that the Council have done me the honour of selecting me to the Chair of Egyptology. In accepting this position, I thank them sincerely for their manner of conferring it, and I hope that I may be able to carry out the intentions of the foundress, and to promote the study of the various branches of the subject. Before entering on details, I should be glad to consult with some of the Council who have had most experience of teaching in unprofessional subjects ... It would be well to consider beforehand in what ways the requisite accommodation might be provided. A room of about 200 square feet would suffice for the library and collection and as a study for readers. But if there should be any spare space at present, I should be glad to make a loan for a term of years, of a part, or the whole, of my own collection, which is mainly technical, and would be very desirable for students. This might fill a room rather larger than the library. I have been considerably adding to the library, on the commission of Miss Bradbury [he had spent on it £250], so that it will be fairly complete. In a few days I hope to call on you and hear further particulars.

The terms of Petrie's appointment, which was regarded as part-time, apparently stipulated that he should normally give a course of lectures in the first and third terms, but be free during the winter months to work in Egypt. This would be in accordance with his aim to use the excavations as practical training for his students. In December 1892 his prospectus and the arrangements for the chair were discussed at a meeting of the Faculty of Arts.

As indicated in his acceptance letter, hard work was going into the preparation of the Edwards Library which was temporarily housed in the South Library and opened on the 12th January 1893. One of its first visitors was Lord Cromer. Kate Bradbury played an important rôle both financially and practically in its earliest years. She began by paying most of the legacy duty on the bequest as 'a gift in augmentation of the endowment of the Professorship'. While the arrangement of the library was obviously due to her, it is equally evident that the antiquities at this stage were still in the remainder of the forty-four packing cases which had arrived from Westbury-on-Trym two months earlier.

Two days after the opening of the Edwards Library, on the afternoon of Saturday 14th January, the new professor gave his Introductory Lecture. Both events were advertised in a special printed notice (Figure 2). The address was open to the general public, and an appreciative audience of two hundred people turned up. In it Petrie was to set out his future aims, both for his new Department and for the expansion of Egyptology, hitherto confined to the study of the language. His words are also a forecast of what his own special interests would be. He stressed the need for part-time students and hoped that University College would become a centre for such volunteers. How gratified he would be today to find a buoyant teaching and research Department with over thirty undergraduate students taking full or joint Degrees in Egyptology. Also to see a flourishing Friends' organization, as well as the indispensible band of stalwart volunteers, both necessary to the running of the much expanded museum.

His appeal in the lecture for funds of up to £400 a year to employ one of his students as an excavator for a season in Egypt was met a fortnight later. A gentleman, whom he had once met in Egypt, promised to donate a sum for a scholarship, the interest on which would be sufficient to pay the expenses of a student on alternate years. Thus his Egyptian Research Account (E.R.A.) was launched, which was to last more than fifty years.

Summaries of the lecture appeared in *The Times* on the 20th, and in a Bristol weekly, but the entire address has never been published. Lady Petrie was working at the time of her

UNIVERSITY COLLEGE, LONDON.

GOWER STREET, W.C.

————— ♦ ■ ♦ —————

EDWARDS PROFESSORSHIP OF EGYPTOLOGY.

PROFESSOR—W. M. FLINDERS PETRIE, D.C.L.

—————————————

SESSION 1892-93.

—————————————

THE EDWARDS LIBRARY, containing works on EGYPTOLOGY, will be available for Students on Jan. 12. This Library will be open, and the Professor will attend to give advice and instruction in the SOUTH LIBRARY, from 10 to 1 o'clock on Thursdays, Fridays, and Saturdays before each of the lectures.

The Introductory Lecture will be delivered on Jan. 14 at 2 P.M.

A course of six lectures on "Egyptian Art" will be delivered on succeeding Saturdays, Jan. 21 to Feb. 25, at 2 P.M.

The Introductory Lecture will be open to the public without payment or tickets.

Fee for a term .... £1 1s.

2. *Printed announcement of the beginning of the first term, January 1893. (Property of the Petrie Museum, UCL.)*

death in 1956 on a project aimed at editing some of her late husband's manuscripts. Included among these was a separate volume entitled: '100 delivered addresses of W. M. F. P.' However, it never came to fruition. The manuscript of the 1893 Introductory Lecture now resides in the archives of the Petrie Museum in a copy typewritten and annotated in her own hand.

As a tribute to the memory of our godmother and her first Edwards Professor, and to fulfil one of the last wishes of his widow, it has been decided to publish it in full in this Centenary volume (Appendix 2).

5

Chapter Two

Petrie's 'Pups'
1893~1913

The new professor was early convinced of the healthy signs of interest being taken in his new subject, and felt that this could only grow if, as he said, 'the public are kept properly informed'. Following his Introductory Lecture, Petrie gave a course of six open lectures on Egyptian art which took place, again on Saturdays at 2 p.m., during January and February 1893 (see Figure 2). He was to write to his protégé Percy Newberry: 'The lectures go very well ... thirty-five last Saturday at the first lecture of the series on Egyptian Art. I use about forty slides to each lecture'.

For the routine teaching he began with eight students, although the system was obviously very flexible. Among them was Margaret Eyre, who was reading for a degree in English. She is reported to have said: 'I date from the days when one just walked into any lectures one fancied'. The students paid £2 12s 6d. for the full session or one guinea a term. Remarkably, these fees did not really increase until the 1920's. Nearly all the first group consisted of ladies, two of whom were married. But there was at least one man: Dr. James Walker, a former medical practitioner and graduate of the College. He would soon become Petrie's main assistant, a situation which lasted until his sudden death in 1914 at the age of fifty-six. Walker is reputed to have been an enthusiastic and patient teacher, 'a real gentleman' who was always ready to give time and attention to his pupils. However, he began by supervising the Edwards Library, thereby solving a serious problem, especially when Petrie was away, as each professor was librarian in his own Department. As yet he took no part in the teaching.

Petrie did not feel confident enough to teach language classes in Egyptian and Coptic, so he proposed hiring Francis (Frank) Llewellyn Griffith and Walter Ewing Crum, both brilliant young linguists, to undertake these respective tasks. Griffith (see Figure 4) had spent four seasons from 1884 onwards excavating with both Petrie and Naville at various Delta sites. In 1886 he had accompanied Petrie on his trip through Upper Egypt. As no post in Egyptology was available to him, he had in 1888 accepted an appointment as an assistant in the Department of British and Medieval Antiquities and Ethnography at the British Museum. Crum was an Oxford graduate who had just spent two years studying in Berlin and was fast becoming an established Coptologist.

The plan for Griffith to teach at the College met with difficulties, however, the Senate refusing to authorize the arrangement. It was stated that: 'Professor Petrie's prospectus be approved with the exception of the clause providing for lessons in Hieroglyphs, Inscriptions, and Philology, which are matters already dealt with by Professor Poole'. The reason for this decision was that Reginald Stuart Poole, Professor of Classical Archaeology since 1889, was an Egyptologist at heart and felt that he should have been asked to teach the language. Since taking over the chair Poole had considerably widened the scope of the courses in his department, paying specialists to lecture for him and so allowing him time to concentrate on his favourite subjects: numismatics and Egyptology. He had been surprised and bitterly dismayed by Petrie's appointment, for a long silence had already grown up between the two men since Petrie had broken with the Egypt Exploration Fund in 1886. Poole, then still Keeper of Coins and Medals in the British Museum, had been co-founder and joint Honorary Secretary of the Fund; he would later become its Vice-President.

6

Petrie, however, was anxious to avoid any friction within the College. Accordingly, in January 1893 he wrote to the Secretary announcing his intention of holding the Egyptian classes, for which there was already a demand, outside the premises as a private undertaking. Griffith therefore gave his lectures on Thursday evenings in Petrie's bed-sitting-room at 32, Torrington Square.

The first class, which was attended by Petrie's closest friend Dr. Flaxman Spurrell, is described in the same letter to Newberry from the end of January 1893:

R.S.P.[oole] got the Council to refuse to agree to my having any teaching in the Language, right in the face of the terms of the bequest! So I quietly withdrew that from the College, and held a class in my own rooms; we started yesterday, F.L.G.[riffith] at one end expounding, and W.M.F.P. acting as chorus. There were eleven in for it, all eager. It will soon have to be moved to the S.B.A. [Society of Biblical Archaeology] room if we increase at all. It is a pretty commentary on the obstructive.

Actually, an arrangement for the teaching of Egyptian within the College would have cost the authorities nothing. Students' fees in those days went directly to their teachers, and the professor was expected to pay his assistants out of his own salary. Fortunately, Walker was well-off so did not require any remuneration, whereas Griffith received the paltry sum of £20 per annum.

In the spring of 1893 Petrie spent two months in Italy recuperating from a serious illness. He took many photographs at ancient sites and of museum objects in order to add to the one thousand he already had and to continue to build up his projected Departmental archives (see Appendix 2). Whilst in Florence he found a marble-worker who introduced him to his supplier, with whom Petrie bargained for alabaster mounts for statuettes. 'I ordered 600 at once, at 1d. to 2d. each, polished, to be sent on to London; and I can order over whatever I want in future for mounting. This is the cheapest, neatest and quickest way of mounting things.' These blocks were still being used in the collection up to the outbreak of the Second World War.

They could be put to immediate use when Petrie returned to England, for in May 1893 the new Egyptology Department acquired part of the top (second) floor in the South Central Building (i.e. above the South Cloisters), newly vacated by the Engineering Department. This would be its home until 1940. The total floor space was 120 by 50 feet, but half this area was initially occupied by the Yates Archaeological Library, also established by recent bequest. A partition wall separated the two.

Amelia Edwards' collection could now be unpacked, and Petrie was able to move his own antiquities, housed in fifty full boxes, out of his family home at Bromley, Kent. It was for some years to be on loan to the College. The Edwards' Collection had been built up in three ways: antiquities that she had herself purchased during her 1873-74 Nile journey; those specifically bought for her by Petrie in Egypt; and some minor pieces which had been granted to her 'for a museum' by the E.E.F. Nearly all the latter had in fact been excavated by Petrie!

Petrie's own collection had been acquired from his share of official divisions when excavating privately from 1886 onwards, and by purchases from dealers. Thus there entered the College in 1893 excavated objects from the sites of Hawara (our forty splendid mummy portraits), Kahun and Gurob (towns which had yielded domestic artefacts), Meydum (some fine painted plaster), and El-Amarna (see p. 4).

In January 1893, Kate Bradbury had offered to provide showcases for the Edwards' antiquities, for only a couple had arrived with the bequest, and, under certain conditions, others for Petrie's loan collection. The stipulation regarding the latter had been that if at any time the cases were no longer required in connection with the Edwards Chair, the College should take them over at cost price 'allowing for all or any deterioration in their value, which may have taken place'.

The unpacking and arrangement of the antiquities in these new cases was undertaken by the indefatigable Miss Bradbury, assisted by Griffith and Spurrell. Dr. Walker and James Quibell, a young Oxford graduate in Greek and Chemistry, came in every day. Quibell was to excavate with Petrie at Koptos in 1893-94 as the first recipient of the Egyptian Research Account Studentship. However, the picture given by Petrie of these early years is that the collections were mainly stored in layers piled on sheets of paper, one on top of the other, in a few cases, two of which were over twenty feet in length. Larger objects were laid out in the ever increasing smut, dust, and wet blown in from the skylights, so that they soon became grey, and pottery was smashed by brooms and scrubbing. It was a hopeless task trying to keep the cases or white sun blinds clean (the latter had been both suggested and designed by Petrie). Space was always at a premium until the move of the Yates Library in 1907 freed the entire length of the top floor for the Department. At this stage the Edwards Library was re-sited, together with Petrie's office, at one end (see Figure 7).

From 1894, after his season at Koptos, Petrie was to move his annual summer exhibitions to University College, the first one being held in the Edwards Library. From 1895 the South Classroom, later known as the Exhibition Room (now the Strang Print Room), was allocated to him during the long vacation. The Department's students were expected to help with the arrangement and staffing of these exhibitions, especially as all expenses were at the professor's own cost. On the first occasion, the portico doors, normally kept shut, were opened to visitors, which made for an imposing entrance; particularly because the large Koptos sculptures, including our famous relief showing Sesostris I running before the ithyphallic god Min, were displayed here. However, in 1898 the floor of the portico was to require repointing since the flagstones had been loosened by the unpacking of boxes containing objects for the exhibition. After this Petrie was instructed that the preparations were to take place in a different area. The same year had seen further protest when the Women's Union Room was requisitioned, at less than a day's notice, for the display. Petrie made a contribution to their book fund in order to 'smooth matters'.

However, the exhibitions were generally viewed much more favourably. The student population was obviously attracted by the preparations, for in 1897 it was reported in their magazine, *The University College Gazette*: 'The excavation of Egyptian antiquities from sundry packing cases in the portico, has for some time excited considerable admiration among a large number of students. We look forward with pleasure to seeing Professor Petrie's exhibition in July'.

A year earlier, at the summer exhibition of 1896, a momentous event had taken place in Petrie's life. One of its visitors had been Hilda Urlin, acting at that time as a copyist for a family friend, the painter Henry Holiday, and temporarily based in the College's Slade School of Fine Art. The beautiful young woman was eyed by the professor 'from room to room' with the result that she started to draw scarabs for him, attended his lectures, and began to learn Egyptian. Within fourteen months she had become Mrs. Petrie. During their fifty-five years of idyllic married life Hilda was to be the loyal helpmate who shared all her husband's activities, and took from his shoulders the burden of fund-raising without which he could not have gone on excavating. For the rest of his life she would be the rock and support on which he could depend.

The yearly displays of excavated objects, which were free to the public, and attended by as many as two thousand visitors, did much to spread knowledge about Ancient Egypt. For the next forty years, 'University College, Gower Street' was primarily to mean to many Londoners - and to others as well - the place they must visit in summer to see Petrie's newly discovered antiquities.

The first loan from the collections took place in 1895 when certain choice pieces went to a three month exhibition on 'The Art of Ancient Egypt' at the Burlington Fine Arts Club, Piccadilly. These were: two wooden spoons from Sedment, one with facing figures of the dwarf god Bes and the other with a girl lutist in a boat; a spoon handle from Gurob with the head of a goddess; and a painted limestone bust of an official and his wife. All four are now on display in the museum. From his own collection he added ten items: five bronze deities; three faience pieces; and two ushabtis. All fourteen objects are illustrated in a plate volume published after the show. Characteristically and correctly, a clear distinction is made between the two collections.

The initial nucleus of the Edwards Library seems to have consisted of the early volumes of the E.E.F., Petrie's early publications; those by Mariette and Brugsch; and the *Proceedings of Biblical Archaeology*. There was not much more. Throughout his professorship Petrie was to place his own books in the library, but they still remained his personal property. He set out to persuade the French Government to donate reports from their archaeological series; and even Kaiser Wilhelm II himself was requested to present the expensive (£33) folios of Richard Lepsius' *Denkmaeler aus Aegypten und Aethiopien* (1849-59). Griffith relates that

Petrie designed 'to a nicety a perfectly balanced book cradle' to facilitate the use of these colossal tomes. It is remembered that it was still in the Department immediately after the Second World War. Griffith had a copy made for his own library, which used to be in the Griffith Institute, Oxford. The readers there did not like it; they felt that it had been devised 'by somebody who either hated books or hated Lepsius - probably both'.

Other additions were to come in the form of donations by the friends of Greville John Chester, as indicated in Petrie's Introductory Lecture (see Appendix 2). This clergyman and collector, who had died in May 1892, had been a friend of both Amelia Edwards and of Petrie. The volumes were placed on a special shelf as a memorial to him.

The library of Joseph John Tylor, known from his work at El-Kab in collaboration with Somers Clarke, was received as a bequest on his death in 1901. However, as many of the books were duplicates, only a small proportion actually entered the Edwards Library, the bulk being sent to Oxford, where Griffith had just been appointed to a readership.

Also in 1901, Kate Bradbury (by now Mrs. Griffith) was showing once more her usual munificence. She offered to complete the library where deficient and to pay for the binding of all the unbound books at a cost not exceeding £100.

Petrie initially requested an annual sum of £30 to keep up and extend what he aimed to be a combination between a reference and lending library. By 1894 it seems to have housed six hundred volumes. In the previous year, in addition to ordering five bookcases at a cost of £50, he and Kate Bradbury had prepared a draft inscription, as stipulated in Miss Edwards' bequest, to be placed over the door of the library. Entrance to it, on the three mornings a week when it was open, was only by permission of the professor. All users had to sign an attendance book and write down their times of entering and leaving. By 1909 a fee of two guineas was levied on all authorized borrowers.

The library was clearly unbearably cold, for a complaint by Petrie in 1898 resulted in the Committee of Management approving the installation of a gas stove in the adjoining 'Philological Room'. Petrie wrote to the Secretary at the time: 'If the Committee approve of 55° I hope you will never warm the Council Room above that for them'. A year later ventilation became a problem. The Committee of Management suggested this could be solved by an electric fan, whereupon Petrie put forward an ingenious scheme for ventilating the library by tubes coming up from the three open windows of the floor below! This was not taken up, so Petrie proposed an alternative plan. The matter was obviously serious, as he could not find any volunteers to work on the collection during the summer because the atmosphere was so close.

Two more bequests were to enrich the chair in these early years. In 1904 all the residual property of Kate Griffith, who had died two years previously, was added to the endowment. A house in Hastings, the Villa Julia, was included, but this came into effect only in 1919 when its resident, Miss Edwards' cousin, died. She had been allowed to continue living there for her lifetime at a peppercorn rent. The sale of the property realized just under £400. In 1912 a second bequest came from Thomas Douglas Murray, an associate of Petrie's, who left £200 to lay the foundations for a travelling scholarship in Egyptology, which bears his name. Unfortunately, the original sum of £1000, stated in the will, had subsequently been reduced by codicil. This meant that twenty-seven years were to elapse before sufficient income (£42) was generated to send the first student recipient to Egypt. The award is one of those still in existence.

As far as the teaching programme was concerned, Petrie continued for some years to give his lectures in the first and third terms on Saturdays at 2 p.m. After 1895 they were always held on Thursday afternoons. They were also open to the public without fee.

In the first term he would lecture on Egyptian history, starting off in 1893 with the Old Kingdom. He was at a loss for a suitable history textbook to recommend to his students, so immediately decided to write a new one himself. The first volume of his *History of Egypt* was published in 1894. It covered the period until the end of the Middle Kingdom, but soon needed rewriting in the wake of his future discoveries. In the third term he would lecture on excavations under the title: 'Various branches of Archaeology and Recent Discoveries'. From 1909 the title was 'Discoveries at Memphis, etc'.

During the First World War the lectures of the first term were replaced by ones on archaeological subjects, in connection with the catalogues he was compiling. Thus 'Rings and

Toilet Objects'; 'Stone and Metal Vases'; 'Button Seals and Design Scarabs'; 'Objects of Daily Life'; and 'Prehistoric Egypt' first make an appearance. Similar matters were dealt with after the War, although social ones then also occur, such as, 'Social Life'; 'Religious Life'; and 'The Official Classes'. The third term lectures at this period were also on special subjects, but from 1920 onwards the theme of 'Recent Discoveries' reappears.

Petrie was not a good teacher in the ordinary sense of the word, for he could not be bothered with the routine work of teaching a class of beginners. He had little time for those 'who wished to be taught, and not to learn'. His lectures, however, were so popular that they often had to be repeated, sometimes more than once, to audiences of fifty people or more. His bold views and clear explanations meant that they were said to be 'quite breathtaking and the audience listened spellbound'. Spontaneous applause was even occasionally heard at the end of routine classes.

His teaching must be viewed against the

3. *Margaret Murray wearing her doctoral robes of 1931. (Courtesy of Miss Margaret Drower.)*

background of some opposition in those early years from various religious factions, since Petrie was believed to contradict Biblical tradition. One student had even been implored by members of her family to give up Egyptology for 'that way lies infidelity'. There was also an outcry against 'robbing the dead', heard especially around the time of the discovery of Tutankhamun's tomb in 1922. It was due to Petrie's continuous promotion of archaeology, both by his fieldwork and lecturing, that these attitudes have gradually disappeared.

Poole's objections over the language classes (reported in the beginning of this chapter) were to be resurrected in the autumn of 1893 when Griffith was permitted by the Council to hold his now twice-weekly classes in the Edwards Library. Unknown to the astonished Poole, a public announcement had been issued to this effect, and the end result seems to have been that both men taught rival language classes this session. In Griffith's class there were at that moment seventeen students of both sexes.

Shortly afterwards, in January 1894, Miss Margaret Murray, then aged thirty-one, arrived to join them. This was solely at her sister's suggestion, because she wanted something to do. Thus, almost by accident, began her life-long association with UCL. She was quick and proficient in the language, which she learnt from Erman's *Aegyptische Grammatik* of 1894, or rather from Breasted's translation of the same year. Soon she took over the beginners' hieroglyphic class, and from then until her retirement in 1936 she carried out the bulk of the teaching. It was she who after some years ran a regular Department during Petrie's annual absences. She rose to the rank of Assistant Professor in 1924, and was awarded an honorary doctorate in 1931, her devoted students clubbing together to pay for her gown (Figure 3). Finally, on her hundredth birthday in 1963 she was to visit the College for the final time and be justly lauded (see Figure 24).

Miss Murray has given us a delightful picture of these first classes:

There were over twenty ladies and two men. None was of undergraduate age. The ladies were all very learned, they had "done" many subjects - chemistry, botany, history, etc. ... Of the two men, one was a retired Sapper Colonel, with views on the esoteric meaning of the

4. *Kate and Frank Griffith in the library of their house in Oxford,* c. *1900. (Courtesy of the Griffith Institute, Oxford.)*

hieroglyphs. Our teacher was F. Ll. Griffith, then still in his twenties and without the slightest idea of how to teach ... Mr. Griffith's method of teaching was peculiar, for he was trying out the new grammatical rules that Erman had evolved. He would write on the blackboard in hieroglyphs a complete sentence from the inscription he was studying, and under each sign its transcription into English [sic] characters. Under these two rows there came the translation; the class meanwhile scribbling for dear life to copy it all down ...

From 1895 it was possible to take language classes in the second term if required, in addition to the first and third terms. Later on the language was always taught each term. There is never any official mention of Griffith, however. After his marriage in 1896 he and Kate (Figure 4) moved to the home of her widowed father at Ashton-under-Lyne. However, he still continued to teach at UCL until 1901. According to Margaret Murray she took over the tuition of the beginners in 1898 and was officially appointed as a lecturer a year later. Walker, who had been Griffith's most promising student, taught language to the second-years. In 1904 he was to be eventually recognized by the University of London as a teacher of Egyptian and in 1905 as one of Coptic. Sadly, Crum, the main Coptologist, was forced to leave the College in 1910 as the result of a scandal with a lady in the Department. They were both banned from the Edwards Library and deprived of their keys: clearly a sign of the times. Walter and Madge Crum later compiled together the standard dictionary of the Coptic language, a work of the highest quality.

The inspiration behind the intensive and extremely practical Training Course instituted in 1910 seems to have been Margaret Murray. With the enthusiastic help of Dr. Walker she drew up a list of essential subjects for a two-year programme involving eighty hours per session. Eleven exams were to be taken at the end and a diploma known as the College Certificate in Egyptology was awarded to successful candidates. (This was the only specialized qualification in the subject that one could attain at UCL.) The fees were twelve guineas for the complete course or seven guineas for each session. The Diploma was to stand the test of time, most of its language, history, and object dating classes being taken over by Petrie's successor in 1933. More lectures were then added, but by this time the fees had also increased to twenty guineas for the two sessions.

This course gave a complete and systematic training in archaeology, and it provided able students with the opportunity for active fieldwork with the professor. In order to deter dilettante applicants and to reconcile Petrie to what he called 'spoon-feeding' students, Miss Murray added subjects such as anatomy of the skeleton, drawing to scale, physical anthropology, ethnology, and mineralogy. Petrie was obviously won over, for he put forward the proposals at the necessary committee levels, and approval was finally received from the Senate.

A printed prospectus was drawn up in which it was clearly stated that: 'A knowledge of drawing and photography will be required by all students for the purposes of the course'. In 1911 the College Committee (formerly the College Council) gave Margaret Murray permission to set up a dark room in a corner of the Edwards Library, and to buy a set of bones for practical instruction. Evidently, the course was launched.

The first complete general syllabus to be recorded is that for the 1912-13 session, which can serve as a fairly typical example. It is divided into five sections with sixteen subdivisions. Classes were held on every weekday. The first section is called History, for which Petrie taught 'Amulets' in the first term and 'Recent Discoveries' in the third, with Miss Murray filling in with 'Egyptian History' in the second. The Language section involved both 'Hieroglyphs' and 'Coptic' throughout the year with Miss Murray (who had taken over from Crum) teaching the juniors and Walker the seniors. Miss Murray also gave a course on the 'Origin of Signs'.

The Art section contained 'Artistic Anatomy', during the second and third terms, by Professor (Sir) George Thane of the Anatomy Department. Also during the third term Petrie taught the 'Dating of Objects'. Lectures on 'Ancient Art' were given by Professor Ernest Gardner, who had been elected, largely on the recommendation of Petrie, to the Chair of Classical Archaeology vacated on Poole's retirement in 1894. The two men were to be lifelong friends and colleagues, Gardner being Petrie's constant ally and advocate, especially when he reached the lofty rank of Vice-Chancellor of the University of London after the First World War.

Then there was Anthropology. Dr. Seligman, of the London School of Economics, ran a course on 'Ethnology and Anthropology' in the first and third terms, and Dr. Derry of UCL one on 'Physical Anthropology' in the third term. A continuous class on 'Manners and Customs' was taught by Miss Murray. Finally, Elementary Mineralogy featured, with Professor Garwood lecturing throughout the session on the 'Minerals, Rocks and Geology of Egypt'.

The only change to this syllabus came in 1916-17 when 'Principles of Organic Chemistry' (involving both lectures and practicals) was added. It could be taken as an optional subject in place of mineralogy. 'Artistic Anatomy', however, disappears after a year.

From 1917 onwards Miss Murray taught the senior course in Coptic after the death of Walker. She also covered religion and social customs. Indeed, her book *The Splendour that was Egypt* (1949) may be said to give in its index an excellent summary of the range of her lectures.

A later example of the general syllabus is illustrated here (Figure 5). In it an Evening School is mentioned, which already existed as early as 1908. This had four lectures: elementary and advanced hieroglyphs ran simultaneously on both a Thursday and a Friday. Petrie taught 'The Dating of Objects' in the third term, and at the other times there would be 'Egyptian Religion' by Miss Murray, which in some years alternated with 'Manners and Customs'. In 1923 a proposal was put forward at a meeting of the Faculty of Arts that three years of evening classes should qualify for the Certificate of Egyptology, but for some reason the recommendation was withdrawn a month later by the Dean and was never resurrected.

Some of the students who passed through the Department during the pre-war years were to make their names in the subject. Together with their post-war counterparts, many of them would show their loyalty to and affection for their professor by the way in which they referred to themselves as a 'Petrie Pup'. Actually, it was a term applied in the early part of the century to those selected by Petrie to act as his assistants in the field. According to one of them they were: 'a miscellaneous lot, culled from different professions having aptitudes and skills in no way connected with Egyptology'. Indeed, academic knowledge was a definite bar to their employment, for as Petrie said in his Introductory Lecture: 'No greater mistake is made than supposing that an excavator must needs be a scholar'. The main exception to this rule was made in favour of those who had joined Dr. Murray's evening classes in elementary hieroglyphs. 'Her sharp eye soon divided the sheep from the goats and many distinguished men started in this way.'

It must have been in 1894 that the fifteen year old Alan Gardiner (see Figure 18), who lived in nearby Tavistock Square, received some language lessons from Griffith in the College. Gardiner was later to dedicate his monumental *Egyptian Grammar* (1927) to his mentor: 'In Grateful Remembrance of my earliest lessons in Hieroglyphics'. Sir Herbert Thompson, one of the leading demotists of his generation, likewise started his Egyptological career with Griffith. He had earlier studied biology at UCL but had overstrained his eyes so that he was forbidden to use the microscope. He was also taught at the College by Crum, and even lectured there himself in the 1915-16 session, after the sudden death of Walker. Miss Emily Patterson was another student of Griffith. The erstwhile friend and private secretary of Amelia Edwards, she took over from her as General Secretary of the E.E.F. from 1892 until her retirement in 1919. Probably this was the reason why in 1898 she was exceptionally permitted to study free of charge.

In 1895 Petrie wrote to Newberry: 'We are overrun with lady students wanting to come out; three of them are good draughtswomen and colourists, and I hope to plant them out at Sakkara and Thebes to copy tombs and hieroglyphics. It will be a great help if we develop a corps of lady artists to turn on to important places'. Two of these were Rosalind Paget and Annie Pirie. In 1895-96 they were

UNIVERSITY OF LONDON, UNIVERSITY COLLEGE.
SESSION 1923-24.

Egyptology

FIRST TERM.

Professor FLINDERS PETRIE, D.C.L., LL.D., F.B.A., F.R.S.

will give a Course of Six Lectures on

(A1) RELIGIOUS LIFE IN EGYPT

On THURSDAYS at 2.30 p.m., beginning October 4th.

SECOND TERM.

Miss MARGARET A. MURRAY, Fellow of the College,

will give a Course of Six Lectures on

(A2) EGYPTIAN HISTORY

On THURSDAYS at 2.30 p.m., beginning JANUARY 17th.

THIRD TERM.

Professor FLINDERS PETRIE, D.C.L., LL.D., F.B.A., F.R.S.

will give a Course of Six Lectures on

(A3) RECENT DISCOVERIES

On THURSDAYS at 2.30 p.m., beginning MAY 15th.

The First Lecture of each Course will be open to the Public without Fee or Ticket.

The following Courses will also be given by Miss MURRAY, beginning as from Thursday, **October 4th** (First Term), **January 17th** (Second Term), and **April 24th** (Third Term) :—

(A4) Hieroglyphs (Grammar)	Thursday, Noon	(A6) Coptic (Grammar)	Friday, 2 p.m.
(A5) ,, (Texts)	,, 4 p.m.	(A8) Origins of Signs	,, 3 p.m.
(A7) Coptic (Texts)	,, 11 a.m.	(A12) Egyptian Religion	,, 5 p.m.

The Library is open to Students on the above days.

FEES.—Any Two Courses ... ... Session, £3 13s. 6d.; Term £1 11s. 6d.
The Course of Lectures, one Course in Hieroglyphs and one in Coptic :
Session, £6 6s. ; Term £2 2s.

EVENING SCHOOL.

S1. (Mrs. Aitken) Elementary Hieroglyphs Thursday at 6 p.m., beginning October 4th.	S3 (Professor Petrie) Dating of Objects Friday at 6 or 6.30 p.m., as required, beginning May 16th.
S2. (Miss Murray) Advanced Hieroglyphs Thursday at 6 p.m., beginning October 4th.	S4. (Miss Murray) Egyptian Religion Friday at 7 p.m., beginning October 5th.

FEES :—S1, Term 10/6 ; S2, S3 or S4, Term, £1 1s.

Tickets are to be obtained at the Office of the College.

WALTER W. SETON, M.A., D.Lit., F.S.A.,
Secretary,
University College, London,
(Gower Street, W.C.1.)

5. *The Syllabus, 1923-24 session. (Courtesy of the UCL Records Office.)*

to work together for the Egyptian Research Account, copying scenes in the tomb of Ptahhotep at Saqqara. The facsimiles of both were used by Griffith in his *A Collection of Hieroglyphs* (1898). In 1900 Annie Pirie was to marry James Quibell and to assist him by making drawings for his publications.

Another female student was Anna Anderson Morton, who had translated one of Maspero's works under the title *Life in Ancient Egypt and Assyria* (1892). In 1902, the year of her untimely death, she published *A Concise Dictionary of Egyptian Archaeology*. This handbook for students and travellers, which has been frequently reprinted, was written together with Mary Brodrick (see page 19), another friend of Amelia Edwards. Mention should also be made of Anna (Nina) Macpherson, a student at the Slade School of Fine Art, who in 1907 was to marry the Egyptologist Norman de Garis Davies and to embark with him on their joint life-work of copying tomb-paintings and reliefs.

The advent of the Training Course came at an ideal time for Petrie, because in 1905 in a lecture at University College he had announced the separation of his work from the E.E.F. and the formation of the British School of Archaeology in Egypt (B.S.A.E.). Its base was to be at the College and, although dependent on the Egyptian Research Account, the new organization had to be much larger in order to support all his own work in Egypt and that of his students. Potential assistants were always needed, and the new diploma course attracted many, for it could be undertaken concurrently with practical work on the Petrie digs. Gerald Averay Wainwright was an early B.S.A.E. recruit, who excavated with the professor from 1907-12 and studied in the Department during the summers. Later he excavated in the Sudan and in Syria, as well as on various sites in Egypt, and became Chief Inspector of Middle Egypt after the First World War. Retiring in 1924, he devoted the rest of his life to his studies, particularly of Egypt's relations with foreign countries, a subject on which he had written his Oxford thesis in 1913.

A group of six who all arrived around 1911 became known as 'The Gang'. Four of them would make an enduring name in Egyptology. They were: Myrtle Broome, Guy and Winifred Brunton, and Reginald (Rex) Engelbach. In the 1930's Myrtle Broome was to collaborate with Amice Calverley in copying the wall-paintings of the Seti I temple at Abydos. Guy Brunton had haunted Petrie's summer exhibitions as a schoolboy, and became a regular visitor to the Edwards Library. His artist wife Winifred made a portrait of Petrie in 1912, which she presented to the College, and another one of Margaret Murray, wearing one of her famous hats, in 1917. Both were painted while she was a student at UCL, and are now housed in the Department. Winifred was later to draw many of the plates for the excavation reports by her husband, perhaps the foremost Egyptian archaeologist among all Petrie's students. She is famous for her water-colour illustrations in two popular books, with chapters by various Egyptologists, *Kings and Queens of Ancient Egypt* (1926) and *Great Ones of Ancient Egypt* (1929). Rex Engelbach assisted Petrie in his excavations over the period 1911-14, and later became Chief Keeper of the Cairo Museum. He had first been introduced to Petrie by a family friend, Mrs. Georgina Aitken, who had also studied in the Department and acted as a volunteer in the collection. In 1919 she was to be recognized as an official teacher.

Finally, there was Sidney Smith, later Keeper of Oriental and Egyptian Antiquities at the British Museum and then Professor of Comparative and Semitic Languages at the School of Oriental and African Studies in London University. One of the most gifted pre-war students in the Department, he attended the language classes of Miss Murray from 1913-14. His son was later to become the fifth Edwards Professor.

Thus by 1913 the Department had developed into an established all-round centre for Egyptian archaeology and philology, as stipulated in the bequest. UCL had been a pioneer both in the initial teaching of Egyptology for students and laymen alike, and in its introduction of the first systematic Training Course for future archaeologists. Two quotations can best conclude this chapter. Professor Sidney Smith, in his obituary of Petrie, states: 'None who came into contact with this Department of London University, for however brief a period, will fail to remember with gratitude the zeal and warmth which differed so much from any ordinary academic atmosphere, the ready help and manifold instruction'. (In this he was doubtless thinking primarily of Margaret Murray.) The second Edwards Professor, Stephen Glanville, in his lecture at the Petrie Centenary of 1953, spoke of the Department as the centre of 'as brilliant a team of scholars in our subject as has ever been found at one time in any single University'.

Chapter Three

Petrie's Pots
1913~1933

From the outset of his archaeological career in Egypt, Petrie had established a reputation for his consideration of pottery fragments, those 'unconsidered trifles' which were to him 'the very key of digging ... the alphabet of work'. Heinrich Schliemann, the discoverer of Troy, when visiting Petrie at Hawara in 1888, had been extremely sceptical of the young excavator's dating and, according to another archaeologist, had expressed himself 'in the strongest terms on the utter impossibility of establishing anything like a chronology of Egyptian pottery'. But 'The Father of Pots', who could put a date to any sherd he picked up, was within a few years to prove Schliemann completely wrong.

Soon after his appointment as Edwards Professor, Petrie had with his 1894-95 excavations at Naqada made the first discovery of Predynastic Egypt (before 3050 B.C.). Admittedly, he did not immediately recognize the culture, which he first thought to be due to a 'New Race', as being so early, but later he was convinced by the French scholar Jacques de Morgan of its real date. A complete series of the pottery was added to his own collection. Later work at sites of all periods of Egyptian history were to supplement this nucleus. It was at UCL in the summer of 1899, by ordering the early wares, that he formulated his famous Sequence Dates, a chronological series, without absolute dates, which was to revolutionize Egyptian archaeology. It can be justly said that our ceramic collection is one of the finest and most comprehensive in the world.

Every year Petrie retained a part of his finds and purchases, although the major items from his digs went elsewhere. His statement: 'I always keep things I do not understand in order to study them at leisure, and sooner or later I find out what they are', aptly reflects his policy.

In October 1907 he wrote a letter to Sir Gregory Foster, the first Provost of UCL, which was to become the turning point for the future of this material. In it he described how for the past twenty-five years he had been purchasing antiquities in Egypt: 'I have always bought unusual things rather than those which can be commonly obtained: hence the collection is largely supplementary to the national collection, and consists of objects for study rather than popular show'. The recent removal of the Yates Archaeological Library meant that space was now available (see page 8). However, this led to the immediate need for a large number of glass display cases. As the minimum estimated cost was £1000, Petrie was not prepared to provide these himself. Nor was he willing to give or keep indefinitely at UCL, a collection 'which represents a very large part of all that I can provide for my family' (his second child had been born a few months earlier). With the firm conclusion: 'I obtained the things for study, I intend to study and publish them in the coming years, and what is to become of them afterwards I wish to arrange now', he put forward three possible courses of action.

The first proposal, which Petrie asked the College to consider, was that it should take over the whole collection and maintain it as a teaching tool, to be kept up by additional purchases. He offered to arrange it during the following year and to 'make a proper use of the materials for College teaching, for which I have long been waiting'. The alternatives were to disband it in parts as he published it, or immediately to send the whole elsewhere and 'I shall remove to that new centre in order to work it out'.

He went on to list what he regarded as the six most important sections of his museum. Essential for practical study were the first three: twelve hundred scarabs with royal and private names, more complete than any other collection; over five hundred strings of beads, the only dated, also the most varied and complete assemblage; and the pottery, similarly dated, and also the most comprehensive series. He then listed the Predynastic material, more diverse than elsewhere, except perhaps at the Ashmolean Museum; the incomparable assortment of tools and technical equipment; and his weights, by far the most extensive group ever brought together. Mention is additionally made of statuettes, stonework, and amulets, all examples carefully selected 'to illustrate variety of work and period'.

Petrie next estimated its value. The £3000 plus spent on purchases, added to the value of the large number of objects from ten years private digging, would total around £4000. Interest on the expenditure amounted to over £1500 more, for in the interim the prices of antiquities had risen exorbitantly, and, due to his knowledge of the native dealers, he had obtained most of them cheaply. Petrie felt that part, although by no means the whole, of this interest should be taken into account, and therefore asked for £5000 maximum as the collection stood at the date of writing, 'which is far below what it would be gathered for now'. The question of any further purchases and an increase in the value of important objects would have to be estimated before any acquisition. In other words, Petrie was offering his material substantially at cost price.

In answer to this letter a sub-committee of four, including the Provost and Professor Ernest Gardner, was formed to consider what steps should be taken. Petrie informed them that, provided UCL made the necessary cases available and performed the required structural alterations in his enlarged Department, he would give the College the option of purchasing the whole collection at any time within five years of the close of the present session. It therefore had until the end of June 1913 to find £5000. Petrie accepted the notion of private fund-raising for this 'among a limited number of private persons and public bodies', but was adverse to using the Press. He further asked for £100 per annum to make purchases and to maintain and extend the museum. The sub-committee duly recommended that the offer be accepted, that estimates be obtained for the cases, and that the building alterations should be carried out during the long vacation of 1908.

By 1912 a spacious museum had been set up and equipped with suitable cases at a cost of nearly £1000 to the College. Petrie now started preparing a handlist of the various categories of objects, for the first time fairly accessible and visible. In May he wrote again to the Provost, reminding him that the close of the five-year option was only a year away. Additions during this period meant that he now estimated its total value at £5985.

The College Committee therefore launched an Appeal to purchase the antiquities at this price, which was far below the market value. By December, Mr. (later Sir) Robert Mond, the wealthy chemical industrialist and patron of Egyptian archaeology, had offered to contribute £1000. He wrote: 'Professor Petrie's Collection is one of the most important archaeological, educational and scientific tools that I know of, and it is of very great importance that it should not be dispersed'. Mr. Charles Hawksley, a member of the College Committee, promised £200. Amongst the minor donors were to both Gardiner and Griffith.

The following April saw the production of an Appeal brochure, entitled 'The Flinders Petrie Egyptian Collection'. Donations were to be sent to the President of the Appeal Committee, HRH Prince Arthur of Connaught. A summary of the objects to be purchased led to the conclusion that it was the best teaching collection in Britain. The Committee also made propaganda for the teaching aspect of the Department, with a detailed description of the pioneer Training Course for the Diploma, instituted just two years previously.

In the same month, while Petrie was still in Egypt, the national Press had been approached and invited to send representatives to meet the Provost. They were handed copies of the brochure, and shown around the museum by the Provost and Miss Murray. Statements concerning the Appeal subsequently appeared in the newspapers, even in some Egyptian ones. A proposed second press campaign in June to raise the remaining sum (the matter was now urgent as only £2600 had by then been collected) was dropped due to Petrie's distaste. In event it proved to be unnecessary, as the same month saw a £4000 anonymous donation, received through Petrie, to complete the purchase fund.

16

The donor was Sir Walter Morrison, a banker and philanthropist. He actually sent the Secretary a cheque for £5000, stipulating that only the £1000 which he had already promised should be acknowledged to him. The remainder was to be strictly credited to an anonymous donor. As Morrison said: 'It is not that I am ashamed of doing this, but a gift, published of £5000 gets into a hundred newspapers, and a thousand begging letters follow. The argument is "Here is a fool, I will exploit him"'.

It was not until the 15th October that the purchase was completed for the sum of £5859 17s 11d. (The odd £9 17s 11d. simply represents interest on the £850 balance, the £5000 having been paid on the 29th July.) Petrie, who had already reduced his final asking price by £135, was anxious about this delay, which caused him complications, for he felt the necessity of altering his will for the three-month interim period.

A formal transfer took place on this date, when Petrie showed the College Committee around the museum. The Treasurer of the Appeal Committee then handed him a cheque for the remaining sum, for which Petrie signed a Form of Receipt. At his request, a note had been added to it expressing his condition that his offer to sell was based on an understanding not to disperse the antiquities in the future. Additionally, Petrie signed a Form of Acknowledgement, stating that the University of London would retain possession unaffected by the fact that he would continue to direct the museum while Edwards Professor. He also handed over a rough census of the objects (any complete listing would have taken far too long to compile), amounting to 25,838 pieces in various categories, with a valuation of each group. No numerical specification was given for the 'large quantity of reserves of inferior specimens', but the real value of the whole was placed at £8530.

Although no mention of the non-dispersal condition had been made in Petrie's original 1907 offer, it was nethertheless 'recorded and observed' by the Senate, a month after the formal transfer. At the same time, Petrie was thanked for offering to the University 'the Egyptian Collection on which so much of his life's work has been spent at a cost not exceeding his outlay upon it'. In December 1913 he was granted his £100 a year to purchase objects, with the proviso that any expenditure above this amount would require a special vote.

Systematic as Petrie was - he is even reputed always to have stirred his tea in a particular direction since he considered this the most effective - he was anxious that precautions against fire and burglary should now be made. Regarding electrical alarms he told the Committee of Management that: 'These should be fitted by a person of known character, as they could easily be tampered with if understood by a burglar'. In the end, alarms were felt to be too expensive and also unreliable. (They were not to be installed until 1988.) Only partial security was therefore possible, although new teak doors, both fire- and burglar-proof, were fitted to the museum in 1914.

Regulations to govern the use of the collection and the Edwards Library were approved by the Senate in November 1913. The main clause was that the Edwards Professor was deemed to be the Curator, unless the College Committee especially appointed another person. Only this committee could give permission for antiquities to be taken out of the building, but the Curator could allow College staff to remove artefacts temporarily to their own departments for teaching or study purposes. Donors to UCL were to have access to the collection at suitable times; as were College students and the public, but these others, by contrast, had to be accompanied by a member of staff and sign their name and address.

In the event a total sum of £6844 19s. was raised by the Appeal. The surplus, of just over £1000, went, at the request of the anonymous donor, to the College Committee to be administered for the maintenance and development of the collection. In 1922 Petrie used £250 of this to purchase objects at auction 'from one of the few remaining private Egyptological collections of importance in this country'. This belonged to the Rev. William MacGregor and was sold in eighteen hundred lots at Sotheby's over nine days.

Petrie's aims and dreams for his museum had been realized in 1913: 'To place it permanently in London is most desirable ... Too often such openings have been neglected in London, and collections have gone to other centres or been eventually dispersed. Such irreparable neglect should not occur again'. He could now concentrate on the material itself and on making it more widely known. In this connection, a request from Leipzig in March 1914 for a loan of 'some stelae and

6. *General view of the Petrie Collection (above) and of miscellaneous pottery (below), 1915. (Property of the Petrie Museum, UCL.)*

season. Worth some thousands of pounds, it was necessary to employ a continuous police guard during its four-week display at UCL. Quoting the exact words of Petrie, the Secretary of the College had written to the Commissioner of Police at Scotland Yard as follows: 'As the main danger is from the international thieves who attack Museums, it would be an advantage to have during the day a policeman who would recognize such men if they visited the place. The guard would sit all day and lie down to rest at night'. In any event, four constables, who were each paid nine shillings and sixpence a day, worked in shifts of eight hours each, the guard being doubled at night.

The exhibition this year attracted crowds twice as large as usual, and nearly three hundred catalogues were sold on the first two days. Happily, all went well and the mishap of the previous year's show did not recur. The electric lighting had then been disconnected at an evening viewing which was packed with people. Petrie had complained to the Provost of this 'outrageous defect' when 'My wife and Miss Murray had to walk round in the crowd of visitors in the dark showing things one by one holding a couple of candles and a single electric lamp for two hours'.

The next year there was no annual exhibition, but on the 7th June 1915 the collection, referred to as either the 'Egyptian' or 'Egyptological Museum' was open to the general public for the first time. Petrie's handbook, constituting a summary catalogue, was ready in time for the occasion. Before this date, interested individuals were only admitted by prior arrangement, which could be 'at any time by appointment with the Provost or with the Professor'. Fortunately, we have an excellent idea of its layout at this date, for Petrie described it in an article, which is illustrated with many photographs. Those used here were

stamps' was approved by the College Committee 'subject to the necessary guarantees of insurance'. Sadly, the imminent outbreak of War presumably prevented this loan from taking place. In 1917, in accordance with his policy, as originally stated in the vital letter of ten years previously, Petrie sold various duplicates, mostly imported ware, to the National Museum, Dublin for the sum of £2 10s. In 1920 further duplicates were to be purchased by provincial museums.

Publicity was to be afforded by the summer exhibition of 1914 which featured the spectacular gold jewellery of the Princess Sit-Hathor-Yunet, discovered at Lahun that taken at the same time, but have never before been published (Figure 6). The account appeared in the 1915 volume of *Ancient Egypt*, Petrie's quarterly journal, published from 1913-35, which provided an ideal vehicle for papers by both staff and students in his Department.

The professor recounts the protracted problems with the new cases. The first batch were made of wood so badly seasoned that they had to be sent away to stop the cracks. The material of the second group warped so that all were returned to be totally remade. These showcases were packed as closely as possible, but arranged so as to be well lit without distracting reflections. Thus the table cases under the skylights were sloped, while the flat ones were placed under the solid roof (Figure 6). A great glass gallery ninety feet long by five feet wide held over a thousand pots. Shallow wall cases, with the light falling through them, housed more than seven hundred necklaces. Each relief was boxed with a glass front panel and top, ensuring direct lighting so that the whole face was fully visible. They were stacked close together to enable a large group of stelae of one period to be viewed at once.

Inside the cases each object was arranged according to its most favourable position with regard to either oblique or diffuse lighting. The crowded displays were purely typological, arranged to show the historical development within each category. Although some labelling and numbering had been carried out, much was clearly still unsorted or packed away (Figure 6).

The skylighted glass roof presented many problems over the years. It caused excessive heat or cold, according to the season, and needed frequent repairs. It was also a security risk, as there were several means of access to the roof, including an iron ladder. An outer trap door, which was abolished only in 1914, even led directly into the museum. The vulnerability of the location caused Petrie much con-

cern during the zeppelin raids of 1917, as even stray shrapnel could have damaged his Department. But the building came through the First World War unscathed; it would not fare so fortunately during the Second.

In 1915 the Edwards Library was sited in its new location within the Department (Figure 7). Then, in 1933, Mary (May) Brodrick (see page 14) bequeathed part of her library to College Hall, the Egyptological books of which were subsequently loaned (in 1969) to the Edwards Library. Back in 1888, Miss Brodrick had been the first woman ever to read Egyptology at the Sorbonne and the Collège de France under Maspero. As an ex-student of UCL (she had afterwards studied under Poole), she had sent Petrie a contribution for the Appeal Fund, and had also given some books, antiquities, and photographs to the Department.

The war years gave Petrie his long sought opportunity to study the antiquities at leisure, and to compile his great typological catalogue volumes, most of which are based entirely on the collection at UCL. As early as 1913 that on amulets was ready in manuscript, to be published the following year. It was the first of what he firmly believed would be 'a series beyond the range of any existing publications, and is not likely to be superseded'.

Twenty volumes were planned, of which fourteen were eventually published, the last two appearing posthumously in one binding just a few days before the Centenary celebra-

7. *The Edwards Library, 1915. (Property of the Department of Egyptology, UCL.)*

tions in 1953. The manuscripts of those on glass, glazing, and dress are now housed in the archives of the Petrie Museum. A corpus of objects, arranged in groups according to type, function, and chronological development, is mostly supplemented with information on relevant technical processes. Each volume is richly illustrated by Petrie's own photographs, as well as by numerous line drawings.

The first of their kind, these works are still indispensable. Several of them have been reprinted in the 1970's. Mention should be made of *Tools and Weapons* (1917); *Scarabs and Cylinders with Names* (1917); *Prehistoric Egypt* (1920); and *Objects of Daily Use* (1927), which are perhaps the most often quoted of the series. By no means merely a list of property, they fulfil their author's aim of forming a library of Egyptian archaeology. Tersely written, they could claim to be masterful summaries of what was then known about particular classes of artefacts. Further catalogues, such as those on beads, sculpture, stelae, figured ostraca, coffins, canopic equipment, and funerary cones have been written over the years by Petrie's successors.

The future of his Palestinian material was to perturb Petrie during the last years of his tenure of the Edwards Chair. It had had to be stored in crates in the basements of UCL, since there was no space within the Department itself. No existing museum was prepared to house and display this unique and very representative assemblage. In 1927, in a lecture to the Palestine Exploration Fund, he stressed the need for a Palestine museum in London with a teaching collection similar to his own. But this did not materialize, and by 1930 UCL could no longer accommodate these antiquities.

At this point Petrie envisaged a large museum running the length of the top floor of the nearby Senate House, the site for which had been newly acquired by the University of London. But the authorities soon made it clear that the new building was earmarked for administrative offices and the University Library. All he could do was to make his need widely felt. Later, an anonymous donor, revealed after her death to have been Mrs. Mary Woodgate Wharrie, made him the promise of £10,000. This Petrie made over to his old friend and colleague at UCL, the archaeologist Mortimer Wheeler, for an archaeological institute for which he had been enlisting support since 1927. The condition

was that Petrie's Palestinian collection should be housed and displayed there. By the end of 1934, a further two years of fund-raising had proved successful and the material was being unpacked at its handsome new home, St. John's Lodge, Regent's Park, the Institute of Archaeology itself being formally opened in 1937.

On the 25th July 1923, Flinders Petrie was knighted 'for services to Egypt', no mention of archaeology being made in the citation. His diary entry for the day laconically reads: '10.30 Buckingham Palace. Knighted. Back by 12'.

Four months earlier, in March 1923, the College student population had put on 'a revusical comedy' entitled 'Flinderella'. Its subtitle 'A Knight in Egypt' would seem to indicate that it was intended to be their oblique tribute to Petrie, whose knighthood had presumably just been made public when the musical was composed. It was evidently also inspired by the discovery of Tutankhamun's tomb which had taken place the previous November.

But, whatever the motivation, the cast list includes 'Philanders Petrie, an Egyptologist', together with 'Lola the Lovely, a daughter of Slade', and 'Sir Grieg Foucester, Provost of the College' (clearly a skit on Sir Gregory Foster). Also listed are 'Bags, Secretary of the College', 'Beedledum, the Beadle', and 'Cantankerous Borenius, a Professor' (Tancred Borenius, who taught History of Art). Minor characters included 'George, the College Gardener', 'Cloister South, detective', 'Cathleen the Camel, a ship of the desert' (played by two actors), and the 'Secretary of the Egyptology Association'.

The musical consisted of three acts, the first being entitled: 'The Provost's Room; a Party', the second: 'By the Tomb of Tutankhamen, Egypt', and the third: 'Meeting of the Egyptology Association, Bloomsbury'. This final act was clearly a direct reference to Petrie's British School of Archaeology in Egypt with its headquarters at UCL.

One of the programmes of 'Flinderella', which was performed for just one night in the gymnasium, still survives in the UCL Records Office. Printed on its back cover are the words from some of the songs, one of which is entitled 'Shovelin'' and has as its initial lines:

Rollin' round the desert, lookin' on the ground,
Huntin' for the treasure, Carnarvon hasn't found,

Dodging Arab robbers, behind the pyramids,
Finding mummy-cases and prising off the lids.

The concluding couplet of this delightful ditty
runs:

But we've chucked all hopes of our degree
Just to work for Flinders P,
Shovelin', shovelin', shovelin' all day.

In celebration of Petrie's seventieth birthday in June 1923, it was decided to raise
money for a Petrie Medal to be awarded for
outstanding contributions to archaeology. Its
first recipient was to be Petrie himself but,
because the sculptor took some time to produce the cast, it was not until two years later
that Prince Arthur of Connaught presented him
with the first copy at a small ceremony held
at UCL. The professor seems to have taken
exception to what he regarded as the medal's
avant-garde design: his own head on the
obverse, with the legend 'William Matthew
Flinders Petrie' around the top, and the 1923
date in Roman numerals below. The reverse
bears the head of Cheops, the builder of the
Great Pyramid, from the tiny ivory statuette
which Petrie had discovered at Abydos. An
ibis, in the foreground, denotes Thoth, the
Egyptian god of wisdom. The inscription
reads: 'Presented for Work in Archaeology'.

The Petrie Medal was thenceforth awarded
every three or four years. Seven distinguished
scholars received it, among whom were Sir
Arthur Evans, Sir Mortimer Wheeler, and Sir
Leonard Woolley. Since 1957 the medal itself
has no longer been presented. Instead, there is
now a Petrie Prize, awarded annually by the
University of London to the best candidate in
the examination for a Master's Degree in
Archaeology.

On the 11th February 1927 the Department
received its first royal guest when Queen Mary
paid an informal visit to UCL. She had
expressed a desire to meet as many women
students as possible, and to see something of
the College buildings. Margaret Murray, as
the Senior Woman Member of the Academic
Staff, was one of those waiting to receive the
Queen in the South Cloisters, and later she
showed her around the Egyptology Department. The occasion concluded with the royal
guest viewing the Refectory where she 'gra-
ciously consented to take tea'.

During her visit Queen Mary had expressed a special interest in Winifred Brunton's *The*
Kings and Queens of Ancient Egypt (see page
14), which had been published the previous
year. A copy was sent to Buckingham Palace,
in the name of the College, on the following
day, as a souvenir of the visit. Lady Ampthill,
who had been the Lady-in-Waiting in attendance, acknowledged its receipt in a letter to the
Provost:

I have received the Queen's commands
to write to you and to express Her
Majesty's very sincere thanks for Mrs.
Brunton's book which you have been
good enough to send from the College.
Her Majesty is delighted to possess it,
and is particularly touched by the kind
thought which prompted the gift. The
whole visit to the College was most
interesting, and the Queen enjoyed it
very much indeed.

Shortly afterwards, the Queen, who had
her own collection of Egyptian antiquities at
Marlborough House, presented 'a carved
wooden figure and a string of stone and
glazed-ware beads' to the Egyptology Department. Miss Murray duly sent her a personal
letter of thanks. The figure is an ointment
spoon in the guise of a swimming girl holding
a duck, whose moveable wings form the lid of
the container. Unfortunately, it has turned out
not to be a genuine piece, although based on
a well-attested type. The beads, which are
authentic, comprise both carnelian spheroids
and glazed steatite barrels, with one greenstone
pendant, and one agate hawk amulet.

In 1931 an important event for the future
history of the Department took place when
UCL acquired Shoolbred's Mews, comprising
two acres in Gower Street, immediately to the
south of the College site. Messrs. James
Shoolbred and Co., the 'Gentlemen's Tailors
and Complete Outfitters' and suppliers of the
College colours, were the holders of a large
amount of land in the Bloomsbury area. They
had gone into voluntary liquidation during the
Depression. Their once-famous department
store, Tottenham House, had covered a huge
block with its main frontage in Tottenham
Court Road.

The Gower Street property, yielding a total
floor area of four acres, contained warehouses,
furniture depositories and factory premises.
Fortunately, all were excellent shells which
had been solidly constructed in the 1890's. In
1945 the Department would move into Foster

Court, the former Shoolbred's warehouse and mattress factory.

There were also garages and stables for Shoolbred's entire motor and horse transport. It was these stables, opposite Foster Court, that were ultimately to become the Department's present home in 1951. Little could Petrie have realized when he employed a professional packer from Shoolbred's in 1901 (to instruct him when packing the Abydos treasures), what a close connection there would later be between the firm and the future site of his beloved collection!

The Department remained open throughout the war years, with the teaching, including the various Diploma courses, continuing as detailed in the preceding chapter. But there were obviously far fewer students. Petrie's re-arrangement and cataloguing of the collection meant that he spent a large part of his time at UCL (often working fourteen hours a day), as did Margaret Murray who was absent only for a few weeks warwork as a nursing auxiliary at the start of hostilities.

After the War new members of the teaching staff arrived, all women. There was Mrs. Georgina Aitken, whom we have already encountered in the preceding chapter (see page 14). She was appointed Honorary Assistant in 1919, and taught elementary hieroglyphs at the Evening School (see Figure 5). In 1924 she was absent for the second term, having joined Petrie's dig at Qau, and her place was taken by Miss Rutherford, about whom nothing seems to be known. Mrs. Aitken apparently disappeared later in 1924, returning only in February 1929 to take charge of the teaching of Margaret Murray who had been granted three weeks leave of absence to lecture in Finland. The arrangement must have lasted somewhat longer, however, as 'the state of ice in the Baltic' delayed Miss Murray's return! At the end of the session Mrs. Aitken officially retired. She had never published on the subject.

Dr. Edith Guest was appointed Honorary Assistant in October 1924. A Doctor of Medicine, she had previously been a student in the Department from 1920, following her wartime service as a medical officer on Malta and in Egypt. She was also a friend of Miss Murray, with whom she excavated on Malta in 1924 and on Minorca in 1932. She wrote five articles in *Ancient Egypt* (from 1930 onwards the title of Petrie's periodical had been extended to *Ancient Egypt and the East*), which

reflect her particular interest in the pathology of the Amarna Period. A sixth, on 'Ancient Egyptian Physicians' appeared in the *British Medical Journal*. In the 1924-25 session she taught Physical Anthropology to the Diploma students, in addition to taking over Mrs. Aitken's evening class in hieroglyphs. After an absence from 1927-29, during which she was replaced for one session by a Lorna M. Weber, she reappears in the 1929-30 session with responsibility for the regular junior course of first-year Egyptian. In 1933, with the advent of Petrie's successor, her collaboration came to an end. On her death in 1942 the College paid tribute to Dr. Guest as a woman of shrewd judgement, kindly humour, and above all, as one who refused to be daunted in the face of many years of ill-health.

Margaret Murray still continued to bear the brunt of the teaching load. She was also undertaking much outside lecturing in order to increase her salary of £200 per annum. Only in 1922 was this raised by £100 to enable her, as is specifically minuted, to relinquish part of these commitments. By 1927 she had attained the age of sixty-five, so could not be re-appointed, as had previously been the case, for a five-year term. Henceforth it had to be done annually, the rules of retirement actually being waived for her during seven years, until the 1935-36 session, once the impending change in headship had been completed.

Foreign students were now attracted to the Department, for example, M. H. Krishna who later undertook an archaeological survey of Mysore in India. Indeed, the last twenty years of the Petrie era produced as gifted a line of 'Pups' as his first two decades. Mention should be made, in chronological sequence, of ten of them, who were each to make a career in Egyptology or a related field. In 1918, while still a civil servant, Raymond Faulkner (see Figure 24) begun his study of hieroglyphs at Margaret Murray's evening class, and it was she who stimulated his life-long interest in Egyptian religion. By 1926 he had become Gardiner's full-time Egyptological assistant, contributing much detailed work to the latter's great text publications. This situation lasted until 1939. In 1951 he began to teach Egyptian language at UCL (see page 72). During the intervening years, he never lost touch with the Department, often undertaking private tuition.

The next three 'Pups' all arrived in 1921. There was the thirty-three year old Gertrude

Caton-Thompson, who soon became firm friends with Margaret Murray who gave richly of her time to the earnest new student. By 1924 the future distinguished prehistorian had already formed a lasting reputation by her work with Guy Brunton at Qau, resulting in *The Badarian Civilization* (1928). Entirely on her own initiative she had found and excavated single-handed the settlement at North Spur, Hemmamiya, still our only stratified key to the sequence of the Naqada cultures of Upper Egypt. Much of the material from that site is in the Petrie Museum.

Thence she set out with a geologist, Miss E. W. Gardner, to survey and excavate the shores and desert fringes of the Faiyum lake. She was digging in Zimbabwe in 1929, and the years 1930-32 saw her pioneer work in the Khargeh Oasis. Later, in the company of Miss Gardner and Miss Freya Stark, this intrepid woman undertook the first excavation in the wilds of Central Arabia. She remained closely linked to her old Department, to which she would leave a most generous bequest (see page 86).

The second student of 1921 was a gifted young Dutchman, Henri Frankfort, who had previously read history at the University of Amsterdam. By 1922 he was a member of Petrie's staff at Qau, and he was later to excavate for the Egypt Exploration Society (the renamed Fund) at El-Amarna, Abydos, and Armant. In 1924 he gained his Master of Arts Degree, awarded with the mark of distinction. He then took his doctorate at Leiden. Frankfort became Field Director of the Oriental Institute Iraq Expedition from 1929-37, and was subsequently Professor at Chicago. In 1959 he was to become Director of the Warburg Institute and Professor of the History of Pre-Classical Antiquity at the University of London. We shall encounter Frankfort again as one of the short-listed candidates for the Edwards Chair in 1933 and once more in 1946.

The third student, Shemuel (Samuel) Yeivin, was the future doyen of Israeli archaeology. In 1923 he gained his Bachelor of Arts Degree in Archaeology and in 1929 a Master's Degree. He subsequently undertook postgraduate work in Berlin. Yeivin excavated first in Egypt and then in Iraq, also contributing much to Palestinian studies. In 1948 he was appointed the first Director of the Department of Antiquities and Museums in Israel.

It was perhaps a year later in 1922 that James Starkey began to attend Miss Murray's evening class in hieroglyphs. His war service in the marines had involved some time on a lighthouse where he was able to foster his interest in reading about Ancient Egypt. He spent two seasons at Qau from 1922, and by 1924 was Field Director of the Michigan Expedition at Karanis in the Faiyum. After seven years with Petrie's British School of Archaeology in Egypt (B.S.A.E.) at Palestinian excavations, he directed his own dig at Tell el-Duweir, site of the Biblical city of Lachish. In 1938 he was to be tragically murdered there in the desert.

Alan Shorter also studied at UCL in 1922. As a seventeen year old pupil at St. Paul's School, he seems to have attended the evening classes of Miss Murray. In 1924 he gained a classical Exhibition to Queen's College, Oxford, where he read Egyptian and Coptic. In 1929 he became Assistant Keeper in the Egyptian Department at the British Museum, a post he held until his untimely death in 1938, when just thirty-three years old.

Gerald Lankester Harding went to Miss Murray's evening classes in 1924, being an office worker at the time. Petrie, forever kind to his impoverished students, gave Harding, who had little formal education, extra coaching. From 1926-32 he was a team member of Petrie's Palestinian expeditions. For the rest of his life Harding lived in the Middle East, becoming Inspector of Antiquities in Jordan and playing an important rôle in the acquisition and preservation of the Qumran scrolls. An accomplished Arabist, he became the expert on inscriptions in the Safaitic script (old North Arabic).

Olga Tufnell became a student in 1930, but had been associated with the Department since 1922 when, fresh from school, she had taken a temporary job as Mrs. Petrie's secretary for the B.S.A.E. Five years later she was still there, and was given her first opportunity for fieldwork when she was sent to copy tomb reliefs at Qau, with four others including the pre-war student Myrtle Broome (see page 14) and Harding. Work on Petrie's Palestinian digs followed, until in 1932 she moved on to Starkey's Tell el-Duweir expedition. After his death, it fell to her to close down the excavations and to publish them, to which she devoted more than twenty years of her life. Her last years were spent on a monumental two-volume typological work on scarabs together with Professor William Ward. She completed and published her part, volume II, just before she died in 1985.

I have been fortunate enough to have been able to talk to, and to record the reminiscences of, the final two of the Petrie 'Pups'. The first, Sir Laurence Kirwan, was a student in 1927. His subsequent distinguished career in Sudanese archaeology has earned him the reputation as one of its foremost authorities. Following work with the Bruntons at Mostagedda in 1929, he joined the staff of the Service des Antiquités, working at the Cairo Museum during the summer months as a conservator, where he helped Howard Carter to set up the last of Tutankhamun's gold shrines. From 1929-34 he directed with Walter Bryan Emery (who was to become the fourth Edwards Professor), the Archaeological Survey of Nubia. After the death of Griffith in 1934, Kirwan became Director of the Oxford University Excavations at Sudanese Kawa, from where he brought the famous Taharqa Shrine, now in the Ashmolean Museum. A man of diverse talents, in his capacity as Director and Secretary of the Royal Geographical Society he organized the 1953 British Everest Expedition, being responsible for its fund-raising, international lecture tours, publications, as well as the daunting task of holding *The Times* copyright against the entire world Press.

Sir Laurence took the two-year Diploma course, of which he particularly remembers the physical anthropology, taught by an inspiring teacher, Dr. Morant (Dr. Derry being at that time in Cairo). The syllabus involved attending human anatomy lectures at University College Hospital where an analysis of skeletal remains from the plague pits of the City of London's Spitalfields was carried out. This was to stand the young Kirwan in good stead when, shortly afterwards, he handled the physical side of all the Nubian burials.

The African Prehistory and Ethnography lectures of Professor Seligman (affectionately known as 'Sligs') were still being held at the London School of Economics. They included those on the Nilotic tribes of the Sudan. Professors Garwood and Ashmole continued to teach their respective subjects of geology and geomorphology, and classical art. Miss Murray had now added pottery drawing and measuring to her curriculum, for which a simple apparatus constructed by Petrie was used. She even gave some instruction in ceramic production, borrowing a potter's wheel for the purpose.

Sir Laurence remembers both Petrie and Margaret Murray as good, clear, and concise teachers. Petrie, commonly called 'The Prof', had not much sense of humour, and certainly did not encourage any undue theorizing or flights of historical imagination from his students. In this connection, one of his favourite expressions, delivered in his surprisingly high-pitched voice, was 'Sheer Froth'. Indeed, his whole approach, according to Kirwan, was that of an engineer or technologist.

He told me two delightful anecdotes concerning his teachers. He would assist Petrie in the preparation of his summer exhibitions, during which the professor would insist on climbing up a rather rickety ladder to pin up drawings and photographs. One day he took one step too many, fell on top of Kirwan, both men rolling onto the floor. It was typical of Petrie that he made no comment, but simply picked himself up and immediately went on with his work.

The second story was about Margaret Murray. She would take the young student to a sparse lunch at Maple's in Tottenham Court Road where she talked about her other passion: medieval witchcraft, on which she was a leading authority. The conversation, revolving around sorcerers, magicians, and the black arts, would somewhat startle the diners at the next table!

Kirwan generally recalls UCL at that time as an immensely stimulating place, of very high intellectual and academic achievement, but there were never any social activities in the Egyptology Department, for the Petries, with what he terms 'their régime of high thought and sparse living' had a parsimonious approach to any kind of expenditure.

The second scholar, Margaret (Peggy) Drower (see Figure 26) bridges the gap between the headships of Petrie and his successor, under whom she was later to take a Bachelor of Arts Degree. In 1937 she became Assistant Lecturer in the History of the Ancient Near East within UCL's History Department, a post she eventually retired from as Reader in 1979. Many of her students throughout these long years were drawn from the Egyptology Department. After retirement she concentrated on her monumental biography of the first Edwards Professor: *Flinders Petrie. A Life in Archaeology* (1985).

In October 1931 she began the Diploma course. Sitting at small trestle tables set up between the rows of showcases, she would draw scarabs for Petrie, which if approved might appear in the next excavation report. According to Miss Drower, the language teaching was rather elementary, Dr. Murray's grammars being used for both Egyptian and Coptic. The 'Origin of Signs' course concentrated on the meaning of the hieroglyphs, sometimes with ingenious explanations from the assistant professor who used big cards with colour reproductions of the Meydum hieroglyphs, which she had painted herself. The skeleton she had purchased in 1911, was still very much in evidence; known as 'George', it was kept in a long box in her room. Students were permitted to borrow bits of it in order to learn the bones. Surveying instruction was given within UCL, triangulations being made around the front quadrangle, and the dumpy level being used up and down the steps of the portico.

Miss Drower stresses the very informal atmosphere in the Department at this period. Most tuition took place around a table in the Edwards Library, Margaret Murray passing chocolates to and fro, and going off on an excursus about witches. A small laboratory at the very end of the museum was used to brew the daily afternoon tea, all contributing to the biscuit supply. But time was moving on and significant changes were in the air.

These were first put in motion when, in October 1932, Sir Allen Mawer, who had succeeded Sir Gregory Foster as Provost, sent a letter to some professors with the information that Petrie (who was now eighty years of age) intended to resign, although he had not yet publicly announced his intention. They were invited to a hastily convened meeting to discuss the implications with Petrie himself, before he set out for his Palestinian excavations. Three days after this, the Provost wrote to Petrie asking him for a formal note stating his intention to resign his chair at the end of the current session on 30th September 1933.

This Petrie duly supplied, stating:

I definitely desire to resign my professorship at the close of the session, next June. I do this partly to get the time needed for labelling and arranging the collection, and I wish to offer my services for that purpose as Hon. Curator without salary. This will also give opportunity for informing the new professor much about the collection. I hope

to thus give the greater part of three summer months during two or three years.

In March 1933 this offer was formally accepted.

In November 1932 Petrie had written to the Provost from Gaza that he would renounce all salary from the 31st March, in order to avoid entering the following tax year. However, as he was still paid at the end of April 1933, he returned the money with the comment: 'It is a tedious struggle to shake off Inland Revenue officials, and I wish to have no receipts to declare or be taxed in this year and future'.

At the time of Petrie's retirement, the College Committee and Professorial Board passed a resolution which provides an excellent summary of his achievements:

… In the College Professor Petrie has built up a Museum which perpetuates the results of his own excavations: that Museum ranks third in this country for the importance of the objects which it houses, and is at the same time unique as a collection for teaching purposes. By his work in the field he has won for himself the undisputed leadership of the archaeological world. The modern science of archaeology was created by him: to him it owes the first formulation of its fundamental principles. His invention of the system of "sequence dating" has been fundamental for the establishment of archaeological chronology, not merely in the sphere of Egyptology but in every branch of excavation. He has invariably set an example to other archaeologists in the prompt publication of his field-work, which has no equal in any country.

On the 6th July 1933, Petrie wrote to the Secretary expressing his thanks for this resolution, and stating that: 'The College has been an essential basis for my work, which was always facilitated by the cordial manner in which it was met. I much hope to continue to care for the interests of the College so long as I may be able'.

Honours, both at home and abroad, followed in the wake of his retirement. In October he was created Professor Emeritus. Shortly afterwards, the title of Honorary Doctor of Science of the University of London

8. *Sir Flinders Petrie in the cloisters at Salisbury Cathedral in 1934, shortly after his retirement. (Property of the Petrie Museum, UCL.)*

was conferred on him, and early the following year he was made an Honorary Fellow of UCL.

In July and August 1934 Petrie sat for his portrait by Philip de Laszlo. That November it was presented to UCL by his friends and colleagues, in commemoration of his forty years' tenure of the Edwards Chair, for the Professors' Common Room. It now hangs in the Old Refectory (see page 68).

A second portrait, painted at the same time for the artist's own enjoyment, was given by de Laszlo's youngest son, after his father's death, to Professor Glanville for his lifetime; this on condition it would afterwards pass to the Egyptology Department at King's College, Cambridge, where Glanville was Provost at that time. In March 1956, Petrie's daughter Ann was to write to Glanville about its future,

the correspondence being triggered off by the recent bequest of the G. F. Watts' portrait of Petrie to the National Portrait Gallery. This her parents had never liked, and Ann felt it would be much more appropriate if the second de Laszlo painting could hang there. Glanville generously agreed 'that he [Petrie] should be properly represented in the National Portrait Gallery and [I] would be willing to see it go there when I die or possibly earlier if, when I leave the Provost's Lodge, I have no room to hang it properly'. A few weeks later Glanville died, but thanks to the liberality of King's College, which followed his last wishes to the letter, the portrait was soon given to and accepted by the National Portrait Gallery.

A third version, called by de Laszlo a rough sketch, was painted for the family. Lady Petrie initially lent it to UCL at the time of the 1953 Centenary celebrations (see page 67-8). On permanent loan, it originally enjoyed an imposing position just outside the collection at the top of the entrance staircase. It has now been re-sited and hangs just inside the present entrance of the Petrie Museum.

In the event, the arrangement for Petrie to act as Honorary Curator proved to be purely nominal, although he is still listed as holding this position until 1938. In August 1934, in the company of his daughter, he undertook a last sentimental journey to the West Country to bid farewell to his favourite haunts, including Salisbury Cathedral (Figure 8). Five days after his return, he departed from English shores for the last time, to settle in Jerusalem for the remaining eight years of his life.

It cannot be denied that for all concerned this was the ideal arrangement. Petrie's successor was to be allowed the freedom to impose his own personality and his own innovations on the Egyptology Department. It meant also that a new era could develop and flourish independently of the commanding presence who had reigned supreme for over four decades.

The indelible mark of the first incumbent of the Edwards Chair has stood out as a beacon during the entire subsequent history of the Department. 'The Father of Pots' had seen his aims in university teaching, as in excavating, realized far beyond his original hopes and dreams.

Chapter Four

Glanville Takes up the Mantle
1933~1939

As early as 1913, Petrie had drawn up a memorandum on his chair, its expressed intention being: 'to put on record the principles which seem to me to control the duties of the Edwards Professor, before any questions of personal choice may arise in future'. It stated that the aim of the teaching was indicated by the original bequest, namely that 'archaeology is put forward, while language is not to be neglected'. Essential also to any tuition was the use of the Petrie Collection, which had at that point been recently acquired by the College.

Petrie further laid down four requirements for the professorship. The holder should have a 'knowledge of Archaeology gained by experience in successful excavations, and shown by efficient publication'. He must have the ability to instruct and interest the general public. Also essential was the competence to teach the language, or to make provision for this to be done. The final requisite was: 'Sufficient private income to supplement the salary'! The first incumbent's conclusion to this record was: 'I have endeavoured to find, or train, a successor with these requirements, but I have not yet succeeded. I hope that I may do so in the next few years'.

By 1932 Petrie had indeed achieved his aim, for, at his informal discussion with the Provost and a few interested professors that October (see page 25), he was able to present his own shortlist of possible candidates for the chair he was about to vacate. This fascinating handwritten document still exists in the UCL Records Office. Marked 'strictly private', Petrie lists some of his former British School of Archaeology in Egypt students and certain others, briefly describing their qualifications. Included are Brunton (and Mrs. Brunton), Carter, Davies (and Mrs. Davies), Engelbach, Frankfort, Garstang, Glanville, Mackay (and Mrs. Mackay), Newberry, Peet, Quibell, and Wainwright. (The three wives were felt to be assets to their husbands' careers, mainly because all were extremely competent draughts-women.)

In a chart, Petrie estimated their qualities under various categories, awarding marks for each. Explicitly, this evaluation excluded the imponderabilia of character and personality; it took into account only the technical sides, such as experience with fieldwork, teaching, and 'museum arrangement'. Knowledge of the language, art, history, the Near East, general science, etc., were also included. By far the highest marks were scored by Engelbach, noted as 'energetic, a good worker, and with great experience in running [the] Cairo Museum'. He was closely followed by Mackay, with Carter in third position. Glanville, said to have a 'good general knowledge' was obviously discussed by Petrie at the October meeting, for an annotation in another hand reads 'more language than archaeology'. He simply falls into the same category as all the remaining candidates.

The Provost, however, had other ideas for the future of the Edwards Chair. Sir Allen Mawer soon determined that less stress was going to be laid on actual excavation work 'although one of the two members of staff should be conversant with it'. Rather, the wealth of the museum should now be fully exploited for archaeological teaching, with language tuition also forming an essential element. Late in 1932, he therefore asked advice regarding possible candidates from T. Eric Peet, the Brunner Professor of Egyptology at Liverpool, and from Dr. Alan Gardiner.

A problem was that the chair was nowhere near fully endowed. Indeed, due to a fall in railway stocks, Amelia Edwards' bequest now brought in under £150 a year, and was expected to decline still further. For many years general College funds had supplemented the income from the endowment to give Petrie more of a half-time (as opposed to an originally very part-time) appointment. He had ended up on a salary of £650 per annum, without superannuation allowance.

Although the vacancy was intentionally never formally advertised, various Egyptologists soon inquired after the possibility of being considered as candidates. Battiscombe Gunn, then Curator of Egyptian Antiquities at the Philadelphia University Museum, was one of them. Another was Ernest Mackay, so favourably viewed by Petrie, who at that time worked in India. Gunn later withdrew his application. A pure philologist, he preferred putting in for the Oxford readership which, following the retirement of Griffith, was being decided in the same year. Henri Frankfort (see page 23) applied on condition that he would only be responsible for the non-philological side of the teaching, and that the field would be extended to cover also the Near East. In another letter he announced that if appointed he would apply 'for naturalization in this country' and renounce his Dutch citizenship.

Stephen Ranulph Kingdon Glanville decided to put in for the post in December 1932, sending in his formal application early the following year. An Oxford graduate, albeit with a Fourth Class degree, he had in 1922 taken a job in a government school in the Nile Delta. Determined to make Egyptology his career, he managed, in spite of many difficulties, to use his time in that country to maximum advantage by teaching himself the basic elements of archaeology and gaining a first-hand knowledge of a large number of sites and monuments. In 1923, after an inspiring visit to the newly discovered tomb of Tutankhamun, he abandoned his comparatively secure employment and became an assistant on the Egypt Exploration Society's excavations at El-Amarna. It was Francis Griffith, who soon became his director here, with whom he began his study of Egyptian. In 1924, on passing the necessary examination, Glanville became an Assistant Keeper in the Department of Egyptian and Assyrian Antiquities at the British Museum, where a vacancy had been created by the retirement of Sir E. A. Wallis Budge. During the following nine years he enjoyed the encouragement of three ex-UCL students.

Sidney Smith, Keeper of the Assyrian side of the Department, was his joint superior. Alan Gardiner assisted him in Egyptian, to be followed by Herbert Thompson, from whom Glanville learnt Demotic, a knowledge which was to be so vital for the final stage of his meteoric career.

Thus three names were now short-listed, those of Mackay, Frankfort, and Glanville. An Appointments Board was already in existence in March 1933, and at the same date the College Committee formally decided to alter the old arrangement of what was deemed a part-time appointment, because one term in each session was spent on excavations. This was considered to be 'not in accord with more recent views as to appropriate terms of appointment to Chairs involving Archaeological work'. Other universities regarded fieldwork as an integral part of the duties of a professor, and the College Committee was gracious enough to concede that until then UCL had been enjoying 'a full-time professor at a cheap rate'. But as the funds were clearly insufficient for the creation of such a professorship, it was decided to appoint instead a full-time Reader as Head of Department, at a salary of £600 per annum, including superannuation. This was to be on a five-year term. Only when the next vacancy arose in the post of Assistant Professor (i.e. when Margaret Murray retired in 1935) would a full-time professorship be possible, for which the then reader would be eligible.

It is therefore evident that Glanville's appointment to a readership was not, as has often been stated, due to the fact that Amelia Edwards had debarred any applicant from the British Museum from holding her professorship, but was simply due to financial considerations. Indeed, during the time the Edwards Chair remained vacant, the revenue from the endowment was not used for the readership, but allowed to accumulate.

It was on the 8th June 1933 that the Appointments Board met to decide on Petrie's successor. Unanimously they proposed Glanville. The explicit reason that Frankfort was not selected is mentioned by the Provost, namely that the College could not afford to pay for the extension of the Department which he required. On the 14th of the same month Glanville was officially appointed. He is shown here in a studio portrait taken around this date (Figure 9). This is the young scholar - he was then thirty-three years old - who would fulfil the Provost's aims for the direction in which the Edwards Chair should develop.

One of the new incumbent's first tasks was to attempt to build up the Edwards Library, much depleted by the removal of those books which were Petrie's personal property. Indeed, in the opinion of Professor Hellmut Brunner, one of the foreign students, the library was largely inadequate. Therefore, he had to resort to the Reading Room of the British Museum, which was possible since he was just twenty-one. Glanville estimated that £130 was needed to rectify the deficiencies. Early in 1934, the Library Committee granted £30 for this purpose, recommending at the same meeting that the contents of the Edwards Library be included for the first time in the general catalogue of the College Library, thus bringing it under the control of this committee for the first time in its history. The remaining sum required came from College funds. In the same year it was Sir Robert Mond, whose generosity had done so much back in 1913 to enable the College to purchase the Petrie Collection, who now defrayed the cost of the new metal bookshelves in the Edwards Library, for which a separate room had now been created. In 1937 he also presented the funds to provide the Department with photographic equipment and a studio.

In 1942 a total of a hundred and seventy-four volumes and pamphlets were donated by Mrs. Nina de Garis Davies, from the library of her late husband. But what was to become the most important post-war bequest to the Edwards Library was mooted for the first time as early as December 1933. At this date Dr. Alan Gardiner wrote to the Provost stating that he was willing to leave his Egyptological library (reputed to be the most comprehensive in private hands in Britain) to UCL, under three conditions. Firstly, the College must take over the responsibility for the hieroglyphic founts which Norman de Garis Davies had prepared for his *Egyptian Grammar* (1927), and which had been paid for by Gardiner's millionaire father. This was gladly agreed to. The second demand was that

9. *Studio portrait of Stephen Glanville at about thirty years of age,* c. *1930. (Courtesy of Mrs. Catherine Frankfort.)*

the original copies of the Theban tomb-paintings by Nina de Garis Davies, which had been commissioned by Gardiner, were accepted by UCL. This again presented no problem, Glanville even having elaborate plans to display these splendid pictures on the spiral staircase leading up to the Department.

The third requirement, on the other hand, appeared to be much more difficult to accede to, as this concerned the future of Raymond Faulkner (see page 22). Gardiner sought a post at the College for his collaborator, but the authorities felt that it could eventually spend no more than £200 a year on Faulkner as an assistant to Glanville. Moreover, the latter was none too keen on the idea, fearing a permanent obligation to a man who had twenty-five or more years of active service in front of him. However, subsequent letters from Gardiner reveal that the future of Faulkner was not an absolute condition, and he makes it clear that he only wanted a part-time teaching appointment for him for a limited number of years. No more came out of this other than a nebulous statement by the Provost early in 1934 of the College's willingness to consider Faulkner in the future for some position over a limited period. Gardiner stipulated that his new will, which would have a codicil bequeathing the library and founts to UCL, would not be irrevocable. Indeed, he did alter it at a later date, the founts being left to the Oxford University Press. Meanwhile, the tomb-paintings had been given by Gardiner during his lifetime to both the British Museum and the Ashmolean Museum. However, the library itself was indeed to enrich the Department after Gardiner's death in 1963 (see page 81-2).

In 1934 the Oxford Professor Emeritus F. Ll. Griffith died at the age of seventy-one. He left a small sum which was designed to supplement the salary of the Edwards Professorship. Unfortunately, since the will dated from 1926, this was still conceived as being on pre-Depression standards. Moreover, it came to UCL only after the death of his second wife in 1937.

Margaret Murray duly retired at the end of September 1935, although she had actually been absent for most of that year, first on a lecture tour in Northern Europe and then excavating with Petrie in Syria. As she said: 'This plan will allow me to retire without any of the painful "funeral feasts" which are so trying to all concerned'. Regrettably, the seventy-two year old lady, who had so long been the soul of the Department, left the College in a state of bitterness. Two years earlier she had written to the Provost: 'I am really staying on only till I see Professor Petrie "safely off the premises", and as he is pretty certain to finish his cataloguing this summer there would be no reason for me to stay, especially as the College is not the College to me any more'. Her unwavering devotion to Petrie proved awkward on the advent of a new régime, although, according to eye-witnesses, the new reader was as considerate to her as possible and acknowledged her strong points. Nonetheless, she once reported him to the Provost because he sometimes stayed behind after hours with a few of his female students when she was not there to chaperon them. Actually, such late stays occurred in order to sort out the collection at a quiet time of the day.

The Professorial Board placed on record its appreciation of all that Margaret Murray had done 'alike for the College and for the furtherance of archaeological research'. Mention was made of the fact that, when Petrie was absent, she had assumed responsibility for the entire teaching and administration of the Department. It was further stated that 'her courageous initiative has led her to undertake independent archaeological work both in Malta and in Minorca'. The resolution continued with the words: 'She will be much missed: by her retirement the Professorial Board loses from its midst one of its most outstanding individualities'. Finally, the Board expressed its wishes that Dr. Murray while she was 'following the brindled cat, [would] continue her researches into the infernal rites of the Witches' Sabbath'. When acknowledging her receipt of this resolution the 'Queen of the Witches' replied: 'I feel particularly touched by the reference to the Brindled Cat'.

In the year of her retirement, the Margaret Murray Prize was founded to commemorate her long association with the Egyptology Department. Its recipient should be a student who had carried out distinguished work in the Department involving the first-hand study of Egyptian antiquities. Together with the Douglas Murray Scholarship (see page 9), the Margaret Murray Prize was first awarded in 1939 and then every third year, for the last time in 1988.

Margaret Murray is remembered with great gratitude and immense affection by all her former students. A wise and witty teacher, two generations of Egyptologists have forever been in her debt. One of them is Professor Brunner, who relates that he is delighted to have seen her in all her glory. He calls her 'a great little person and very impressive'. She attempted to teach him Coptic although, as he states, the greater part of every hour tended to pass with her presenting less Coptic grammar than in telling anecdotes about Petrie and his excavations, continually spiced with gossip directed against Lady Petrie. She also talked a great deal on her pet hobby-horse, namely her excavations on Minorca, for she regarded this island as the central point of Mediterranean prehistory. Once, when he was sitting opposite her at her desk, she grubbed in her pen tray in front of her and presented him with a small blue faience Sekhmet amulet which he treasures to this day. It was his first antiquity.

Brunner's statement that 'in every conversation and when teaching she was extremely kind', was confirmed by Dr. M. Veronica Seton-Williams who recalled the infinite friendliness Dr. Murray showed her as a young and impecunious Australian student. At weekends this indefatigable septuagenarian, who still walked at tremendous speed, took her to places of interest such as Hampton Court Palace and Windsor Great Park. Eventually, she handed over her class at the City Literary Institute to Dr. Seton-Williams when she became too old to continue teaching.

Margaret Murray's many evening classes are remembered by Professor J. Martin (Jack) Plumley. He once asked her why she spent so much time with her pupils who all seemed to be old ladies. She had so much to do in terms of research and publishing, whereas they, by contrast, were never going to be Egyptologists and were not even particularly interested. The witty retort was: 'Ah, my dear, the important thing is: when I've got them here, they can't get into mischief'. Her encouragement of all students, even the miscellaneous crowd of elderly ladies, was noteworthy, as was her endless patience. It is indeed remarkable that, in between all her duties, Margaret Murray still managed to produce such an enormous output of high quality studies.

It was in 1935 that Glanville claimed the title of Professor, which was conferred on him on the 5th November; a significant date as it was exactly forty-three years to the day since Petrie had been appointed as the first holder of the Edwards Chair. His salary was to be £1000 per annum, but this was provided out of College funds, no mention at this point being made about the Edwards endowment. By 1937 Glanville had become Dean of the Faculty of Arts, and in the same year he was also placed on the Grants and Loans, and the Appointments and Promotions Committees. Two years later he was additionally serving on the Library Committee. All this gives an inkling of his talent as an administrator. Glanville had the ability to see, almost at a glance, a problem in all its aspects and implications, and then to find the best solution in the shortest time. No matter was too small to escape his attention. For example, in 1937 he complained, together with the Professor of Archaeology, 'as to the smell of cooking in their departments', which was rising by way of a disused staircase between the Exhibition Room and the Octagon. The College Committee took the decision to partition off the lower portion of the offending area and to instal an exhaust fan, which presumably remedied the situation for no further protests were heard. Glanville's flair for getting various types of people to work harmoniously together was the reason why he was so constantly in demand for all kinds of committee work. This meant that he was an extremely busy man. Yet, he always found time to help his pupils in their studies.

As professor and mentor he was universally much loved, one of his former students even referring to him as 'the kindest creature that ever lived'. Professor Brunner calls him 'a lively, permanently jolly man, who was more like a *Lausbub* [rascal] than a professor. He always retained the middle course between personal attention and familiarity on the one hand, and detachment on the other - he was a good example of a "well-educated" gentleman'. He ran the Department as an informal and friendly place, although with a tough approach, as he both expected and obtained results. The harmonious atmosphere was obviously due to the leadership from above. The former students I have spoken to recognize this as a very happy period in their lives, and feel that they were more involved and self-contained within the Department than was the case elsewhere in College. The prevailing atmosphere is summed up by Professor Brunner in the words: 'In that time the atmosphere in Egyptology at UCL was endlessly old-fashioned, very English, and *gemütlich*'.

Glanville was a man of immense and often devastating charm. He would spare no effort in trying to enlarge the general cultural background of his students. Brunner recalls how he once invited them to his old Oxford College (Lincoln) where he was now a Fellow, a first visit to this city of dreaming spires, which made a deep impression. Here their teacher had his own set of comfortable rooms, containing a good working library, as well as his own servant. After an excellent dinner, he took his UCL pupils on a guided tour of Lincoln, where the Hall made even more of an impression than the rowing boats which Glanville himself liked so much. He also explained the typical workings of the College, but the technical language of such an alien institution, so familiar to his friends, was rather beyond the comprehension of this young German student.

An extremely gregarious person (his memberships ranged from that of 'Ye Sette of

Odd Volumes', one of London's most exclusive and well-established dining clubs, to a local group of Morris dancers), Glanville would sometimes also invite his charges to dinner parties at his London home in Highgate. Here as a perfect host, albeit not on a superficial level, he managed to bring together, from his wide circle of friends and acquaintances, guests with common interests, and was able to promote the Department in this way. The greatest tribute to him may be that so many of his pupils speak of their professor as having been a good and sympathetic friend throughout the remainder of his all too brief life.

Glanville is also remembered as an extremely proficient lecturer who 'could have taught anything, even things he knew nothing about, because he was a good teacher'. Perhaps his greatest gift was the sense of confidence in their own ability which he inspired in his students. He would make them work for themselves, a policy which at least one of them used to equally good effect when he himself later became a professor. Glanville would encourage them to choose their own essay topics - such as 'the pull-saw' or 'babies' - which had to be read out for critical but sympathetic assessment in class. He expected the same high standards of accuracy and diligence as he set for himself, and, never the most patient of men, his precise nature would not hesitate to show in his irritation when he detected carelessness, often to the offending student's lasting discomforture. This developed their self-reliance and also trained them in research methods but, at the same time, saved him a certain amount of work. On the other hand, it is indeed remarkable just how much of the teaching load Glanville alone carried, principally by means of individual tutorial classes. Equally conspicuous is his many-sidedness, for he was proficient in all stages of the Egyptian language, as well as in archaeology, history, and religion.

The extent of his courses can immediately be seen from the syllabus for the new reader's first year, namely the 1933-34 session, even though at this period Margaret Murray was still fully in evidence. There are three main components, the first being the General courses which comprised Glanville's 'Egyptian History', together with Dr. Murray's 'Egyptian Art' (only four lectures). In the Language division, he taught both the junior and the senior 'Egyptian Language (Hieroglyphic)',

with Dr. Murray covering 'Coptic', 'Coptic Texts', and the 'Origin of Signs'. (Glanville never offered Demotic.) The Archaeology section included Glanville's 'Dating of Objects' and 'Social Organization', together with Dr. Murray's 'Egyptian Technology'. There was a course on 'Physical Anthropology' by Dr. K. de B. Codrington, the Keeper of the India Museum (now The Indian and South-East Asian Collection of The Victoria and Albert Museum, London) and Honorary Lecturer in the Department of Archaeology at UCL. Finally, Professor King, Garwood's successor in the Geology Department gave a series of demonstrations on common minerals and rocks in the first and second terms, while Professor Ormsby and Mr. Hart of the Geography Department ran a course of approximately twenty lectures in surveying.

The Evening School continued, with Glanville taking the senior 'Egyptian Language', and Dr. Murray the juniors. She also taught 'Egyptian Religion'. The change in terminology from the Petrie era 'Hieroglyphs' to 'Egyptian Language' is characteristic for Glanville as a philologist. According to his students, he introduced Sethe's *Lesestücke* (1924), and, for Late Egyptian, Erman's *Neuaegyptische Grammatik* (2nd ed., 1933) and Gardiner's *Late-Egyptian Stories* (1932), from which 'Wenamun' was read. Some hieratic was taught, with 'The Shipwrecked Sailor' as the main set text. It was taken for granted that they could cope with German.

From the 1934-35 session onwards, the effect of the change in headship is fully visible. Egyptology now formed part of the syllabus for both a Bachelor of Arts Honours Degree in Archaeology, and for the Academic Diploma in Archaeology. The former was normally spread over three sessions but could, in certain circumstances, be completed in two. The latter was also taken in two sessions. Apart from these, the Diploma in Egyptology still continued. It was Glanville who encouraged his students to provide themselves with either the Degree or one of the Diplomas, saying with his usual perspicacity: 'You may want a piece of paper some day'.

The external examiner for the Department was Battiscombe Gunn. In 1933 he had not been successful in his application for the Oxford readership, but a year later he had taken over as professor after Peet's sudden death. Gunn is remembered by Margaret Drower for awarding her a First Class Honours

Degree, despite her treatment of the Old Perfective which he did approve of; and by another student for reproaching Glanville for not making the Diploma in Egyptology a degree course as it 'was worth an Oxford B. Litt.' Indeed, there existed some bitterness about the lack of a pure Egyptology Degree.

After the retirement of Margaret Murray, all courses were evidently taught by Glanville. Apart from Middle and Late Egyptian and Coptic, there were 'Social Organization and Religion', 'Egyptian Art', 'Historical Sources for Special Periods', and 'Epigraphy and Palaeography'. 'Elements of Physical Anthropology for Archaeologists' was now taught by Dr. Una Fielding of the Anatomy Department, and 'Elements of Technology' by Dr. K. de B. Codrington. The latter is recalled as a competent instructor, who dealt, for example, with metal casting, and used objects from a wide variety of cultures, including many from the Nile Valley.

During their studies the undergraduates followed two more courses: 'Museum Technology' and 'Dating of Objects and Technology'. The former comprised six introductory lectures plus seminar classes and demonstrations. It had previously been taught by Dr. Murray, during whose absence in 1935 Dr. J. H. Plenderleith, Head of the British Museum's Research Laboratories, gave three lectures. It was then taken over by Glanville. The latter was his favourite topic, for it reflected his whole belief, as presented to one student at her initial interview: 'If you really want to do Egyptology, the collection makes it an ideal place to do that'. He would encourage his pupils time and again to make use of the privilege, whether from the fact that the cases were permanently open or because the keys stuck, that the artefacts were easily accessible. Professor Brunner for instance can still hear his admonition: 'Handle the objects, handle them!' He says, they were instructed that 'we should always touch the original objects, feel them, in order to get to know the material and to recognize the traces of their manufacture. Also to hold them so that they caught the right light, which used to be a problem in view of the poor lighting. Every museum director would get the creeps at this freedom - we enjoyed it'. Dr. I. E. S. Edwards likewise experienced Glanville's teaching methods, with a complete course on scarabs which made a particular impression. 'I remember we spent the first lecture learning to identify materials;

I had never heard of steatite and several other stones. We then had a number of lessons on type and dating, all held in the Museum handling the scarabs.'

Glanville's students regarded these 'Dating of Objects and Technology' classes as 'both a peak and a crunch'. In the first-year, he explored with the actual objects, in the Petrie Museum or by using the galleries of the British Museum, Egyptian art and architecture, crafts and agriculture. Using any class of artefact and implement, he was able to give a clear and convincing exposition of the information they could divulge about the life, work, and even the social problems, of those who had used them so many millennia ago. In the second-year the crunch came, for the students were no longer told but asked about the techniques. 'What period was this carved, and why do you think so?' 'What aspects of the art point to the period of this carving and why?', and so forth. Although painful, this was an excellent introduction in depth to the history of Egyptian civilization, and the professor imparted a vivid picture to all who heard him.

Attendance at extra-mural lectures was also encouraged, such as those by Leonard Woolley, the excavator of Ur, held at the Courtauld Institute of Art. Glanville himself continued a Petrie tradition by giving a course of three public lectures on 'Recent Excavations in Egypt' in February 1937 (Figure 10). After the retirement of Margaret Murray and until the end of the 1937-38 session, Glanville also had sole responsibility for the Evening School. For this, only 'Egyptian Language' is now mentioned, for juniors as well as for seniors.

It was in the autumn of 1936 that Glanville managed for the first and only time to take advantage of the terms of his appointment, which categorically allowed him to be absent for one term in each year 'for purposes necessary to the work of the Department'. He took two of his students together with Miss Violette Lafleur, a voluntary worker in the museum whom we shall encounter shortly, and went with them to Egypt, where they visited the excavations at both El-Amarna and Armant. On the outward journey this ardent museum man had insisted they should stop off to view the great Egyptological collection at Turin. A later leave of absence granted to Glanville in order to visit Egypt from mid-November 1939 till the end of the following spring term had, regrettably, to be cancelled on

Department of Egyptology.

A Course of Three Public Lectures

on

RECENT EXCAVATIONS IN EGYPT

will be given by

Professor S. R. K. GLANVILLE, M.A., F.S.A.,

on

Friday, February 5th, 12th and 19th, 1937,

at 5.30 p.m.

I. Feb. 5th. Background to contemporary excavations; scientific aims in the field to-day. Excavations of the prehistoric and archaic periods; Saqqarah: Hemaka and Zoser.

II. Feb. 12th. The Old and Middle Kingdoms: Gizah, Saqqarah, Fayūm, Karnak, Armant, Tūd.

III. Feb. 19th. The New Kingdom and the last phase of Egyptian culture: Thebes, Tell-el-Amarna, Ballana and Qustul.

The Lectures, which will be illustrated with lantern slides, are open to the public without fee or ticket.

C. O. G. DOUIE,
Secretary,
University College, London
(Gower Street, W.C. 1).

10. *Printed announcement of a course of public lectures by Professor Glanville, February 1937. (Courtesy of the UCL Records Office.)*

the outbreak of the War.

In 1936 it was Mr. (later Dr.) I. E. S. Edwards (see Figure 18), a former student of Glanville in the Department (see page 38), who as a young twenty-seven year old, took over the professor's teaching commitments for this one term. He told me that he taught Egyptian, together with some archaeology. The classes were held on two or three evenings a week, for he was unable to get away during the daytime from his post as Assistant Keeper in the Department of Egyptian and Assyrian Antiquities at the British Museum. We shall meet Dr. Edwards again later on in our story and there trace his subsequent close relations with UCL.

Back in 1935, Glanville had received a new full-time member of staff in the person of Miss Florence Mackenzie. She was appointed Departmental Assistant, which really implied that she was Glanville's personal secretary. By the 1938-39 session she was giving the junior evening class in Middle Egyptian, until her resignation at the end of September. During the War she would act as secretary to King George VI's Private Secretary at Buckingham Palace.

The senior course in Egyptian at the evening class for the same session was given by a second staff member, Dr. Elise Baumgärtel, who taught it again in the following academic year. Dr. Baumgärtel had studied Egyptology under Sethe in Berlin, which had given her a sound philological training. Previously, in 1927, she had received a doctoral degree in Prehistory at the University of Königsberg (East Prussia), with a thesis on the Neolithic Period in Tunisia. Afterwards she had worked at Berlin and Vienna, received a scholarship to study in Paris and Toulouse, and taken part in the German dig at Hermopolis. Subsequently, she conducted her own excavations in Italy and the Balkans. In 1933, the year of Hitler's seizure of power, all her German grants were withdrawn, and a year later she fled to England. In 1936 she began her voluntary work in the Petrie Museum, spending three days a week in registering and rearranging the Prehistoric and Early Dynastic material. Dr. Baumgärtel also taught these subjects in tutorial and seminar classes from 1936-38, her appointment as an Honorary Research Assistant being confirmed in May 1937. In the autumn of 1939 she gave a course of three public lectures on Prehistoric Egypt.

The third member of staff was Miss Violette Lafleur (see Figure 15), a Canadian

11. *Violette Lafleur in her laboratory; the remains of Jeremy Bentham are lying on the table, 1939. (Courtesy of Mrs. Lucia Turner.)*

citizen. The daughter of a leading Montreal judge, she had previously been a social worker in the slums of that city. Her associations with the College had begun in 1933 when, as a devoted family friend of Glanville, his wife Ethel (with whom she had been at the Grove School in Highgate), and their two young daughters, she became a non-degree student in the Department. After two years she started to work in the museum, first as a general assistant, later on specializing in the restoration of antiquities. In 1935 she started her conservation training under Dr. Plenderleith at the British Museum, and in the future she always received considerable assistance from his department. From 1936 onwards she took charge of this aspect of the museum's work, treating nineteen hundred objects in this one year alone. It has been mentioned above (see page 33) that she was one of the three people taken by Glanville to Egypt in the autumn of the same year. Thanks to him, she was able to spend a large part of her visit most profitably working under Alfred Lucas, the well-known Honorary Consulting Chemist to

the Service des Antiquités, who was based at the Cairo Museum.

Miss Lafleur later also became responsible for the photography in the Petrie Museum. From 1939 onwards she received the official title of 'Honorary Museum Assistant'. In this capacity she gave yearly six lectures, with practical demonstrations, on the restoration and preservation of objects, with an emphasis on Egyptian antiquities. The course was popular among the students, who recall her 'incredible gift with her hands' and her sound knowledge of the subject, which she managed to convey in the face of extreme nervousness. Together with an inability to impart information at a basic level, this prevented her from obtaining the rank of a first-rate teacher.

One interesting matter should here be briefly recorded. Just before the War, Miss Lafleur undertook the restoration of Jeremy Bentham, the College's auto-ikon of its spiritual founder, which she carried out in her laboratory in the museum (Figure 11). After his very dirty and moth-eaten clothing (right down to the under-drawers and under-stockings) had been successfully cleaned by a professional firm, Miss Lafleur treated them with a solution guaranteed to render fabrics unpalatable to insects. The original padding of the skeleton, which had been crudely done, was also renewed, after measurements supplied by Dr. Una Fielding (see page 33). The wax mask, received with a thick covering of dirt, together with the straw hat, stick, and chair, were all successfully treated. One student particularly remembers Miss Lafleur cleaning the hair of this mask which stood in her room for some while, having initially caused the cleaner a considerable shock!

Violette Lafleur remains in the memory as a 'tremendous worker' who, although only a volunteer, always undertook a full week, taking only half an hour for lunch. She would usually come in even on Saturday mornings. One post-war student feels that a great deal of the administration within the Department, for which the professor got the credit, was in fact done by Miss Lafleur. The title conferred on her by the College Committee in July 1939, at Glanville's request, was felt to be a suitable one for her anomalous position. We shall encounter this loyal, intelligent, and hardworking lady later on in our story when she played a leading and solitary rôle during the War and its aftermath.

A new student in those pre-war days would approach the Department via the many steps winding up from the area between the Cloisters to the second floor. A door at the top opened into a small well-lit hallway with the Sesostris I relief (see page 8) on its south wall. Opposite it, double glass doors led into the museum. The Edwards Library was adjacent to the hall, being merely a small room overlooking the front quadrangle. Glanville's office was opposite, together with a room for Florence Mackenzie. Here in the attics, the entrants discovered a little world of its own, described by one of them as 'quite exciting, like an artist's atelier'. It even 'exuded an all-pervasive glorious musty feeling, as if straight out of an Egyptian tomb'.

Friday afternoon was the time when the whole Department congregated and Glanville talked about the latest finds or on a new text, usually with slides. Miss Mackenzie would produce toasted crumpets for the group sitting around the table in the library. These happy, argumentative, and hilarious gatherings form the fondest memories for Sheila Puckle, who was a student from 1936-39. Aged seventeen and straight from school, the Department was to her an entirely new and fascinating world, of which she claims to have loved every minute. She and one other girl were pioneering the very difficult Degree in Ancient and Medieval History, covering an extensive period from 4000 B.C. to 1500 A.D. She concentrated on Egyptology but was the only person in the Department who had never been to Egypt. Nethertheless, Glanville's teaching gave her a first-hand impression of the country. Later, during the War, Sheila Puckle exchanged her 'entrancing experience' for the violent real world of the armed forces. She was to make the Territorial Army her career for the next thirty years, having been responsible after 1945 for drafting the terms of duty for the regular women's services. A far cry from Egyptology!

The Department was also a cosmopolitan community, attracting a large proportion of foreign students. Some of these were exotic personalities, such as the black American wife of the famous Shakesperian actor and singer Paul Robeson, immortalized for his rendition of 'Ole Man River' in the musical 'Showboat', which enjoyed a long run at Drury Lane in the thirties. Also present was Madame Rambova, the widow of the great star of the silent screen, Rudolf Valentino. In 1946 Natacha Rambova began her collaboration with Alexander Piankoff, who then lived in Egypt. She edited for him various volumes in the Bollingen series, such as those on the tomb of Ramesses VI, the shrines of Tutankhamun, and on mythological papyri.

Then, there were three Germans who later made a name in Egyptology. The first, Hellmut Brunner, studied at UCL for two terms from October 1933 to March 1934. He was to become Professor of Egyptology at Tübingen. His main purpose in coming to London was to learn English, for 'to be a good Egyptologist without knowing that language was impossible'. He took all Glanville's classes and studied Coptic with Margaret Murray, as noted above. Professor Brunner considers that he profited greatly from his stay, for together with his experiences at UCL, it also afforded him the opportunity of meeting eminent Egyptologists, such as Alan Gardiner, and Aylward Blackman and his sister Winifred. It further gave him a general introduction into the vagaries of English life: its mentality, customs, and humour. So many new experiences would leave a lifelong impression.

Günter Rudnitzky spent two years in the Department, from 1933 to 1935, and took the Diploma in Archaeology. Back in Germany he started work on his doctoral thesis about the Eye of Horus. The outbreak of the Second World War led to a failed attempt to flee his homeland. Landing at Hastings with his thesis, largely in hieroglyphs, in his luggage, he was sent back to Germany for the duration of the War, in the absence of an enlightened customs officer who realized the nature of these signs. Happily, he survived military service during the War followed by his captivity. He reports: 'the thorough grounding in Egyptology which I received in this Department helped me in the following dreary years to remain mentally active, and later on to finish my concluding course of studies rather quickly'. He received his doctorate in Mainz in 1952. Later he became librarian at Heidelberg, and, with Dr. Günter Burkard, was responsible for the publication of the catalogue of the Egyptological library at that University.

Käthe (Kate) Bosse was already a postgraduate student, having obtained her doctorate at Munich in 1935 with a dissertation on the human figure in the sculpture of the Late Period. She arrived at UCL in July 1937 with a six-month grant from the Society for the Protection of Science and Learning to carry on her research into Egyptian iconography, for which her training in classical archaeology made her well-equipped. On Glanville's recommendation, this grant was renewed for a further six months in January 1938, but on its expiry she left the College.

During her time in the Department, Dr. Bosse took seminar classes on several occasions when the professor was absent, a task she carried out, according to him, 'efficiently and with enthusiasm'. She also classified and registered objects in the Petrie Museum, rearranging their exhibition for teaching purposes. This experience was to prove a useful training for her future career. She later married the Welsh Egyptologist J. Gwyn Griffiths, who became Professor of Classics and Ancient History at University College, Swansea. Dr. Bosse-Griffiths now acts as Honorary Curator of The Wellcome Museum within this department, a collection she herself largely organized. She has also become a leading figure in the Welsh nationalist movement.

Xia Nai (Mr. Shiah) arrived at UCL from China in 1936 knowing no English whatsoever. This presented no handicap in studying Egyptology, for he found hieroglyphs easy, and his familiarity with pictographic writing enabled him to draw the most exquisite signs which he literally painted. He was later to translate Egyptian into English in a much more down-to-earth, un-Gardinerian fashion than the rest of his fellow students. This, they felt, was probably much nearer to the real meaning, and they were generally entranced by his whole approach to the ancient texts. To them he remained 'Mr. Shiah' throughout, and is remembered by one of them as: 'the most smilingly imperturbable person I have ever met'.

Mr. Shiah himself recalled with humour and self-deprecation how he arrived at Mortimer Wheeler's dig at Maiden Castle in these early days, wearing one of the two western suits he had had made for his visit to Britain. He was immediately told by the field director to retire and change into something more suitable. After a qualifying year, he then worked on excavations at Armant in Egypt and Tell el-Duweir in Palestine, before obtaining his Master of Arts Degree in 1939. In 1946 he was awarded his doctorate, the subject of his important, but unfortunately unpublished, thesis being a study of Ancient Egyptian beads based on the Petrie Collection.

Back in his native land, Xia Nai became one of China's leading archaeologists. From 1958-1982 he was the Director of the Institute of Archaeology at Peking. This gave him overall responsibility for fieldwork in the entire country at what was an immensely important period, with the discovery of the famous terracotta warriors from the tomb of the First Emperor. He himself excavated in several parts of that vast territory, and wrote on a wide range on subjects from coinage, jade, and silk textiles to Chinese astronomy and the zodiac.

Professor Xia Nai was always concerned with maintaining foreign links, not least with Britain. He travelled widely to attend international meetings. In 1972 he presided over arrangements for the great Chinese Exhibition held in Paris and London, accompanying it to both these venues. His last visit to his old Department took place just a few months before his death in 1985, when I had the privilege of meeting this remarkable man and showing him around the collection in which, albeit in another location, he had passed so many happy hours as a young student.

Amongst the earliest British students in

1933 were Margaret Drower (see page 24-5), now taking a degree, and two part-timers, Jack Plumley and Eiddon Edwards, whose first contact with the Department actually goes back to a period five years earlier. As pupils at Merchant Taylors' School they, together with Donald Coggan, the future Archbishop of Canterbury, were members of the Hebrew class which was invited to a viewing of Petrie's Palestinian exhibition of 1928. Here they remember seeing the great man himself, whom they describe as having the appearance of an 'old lion'. He hardly spoke, but his piercing eyes succeeded in following the group of schoolboys around the room.

J. M. Plumley, by 1933 a curate in London's Hackney district, took, for his own interest, Egyptian with Glanville and pottery drawing with Margaret Murray. The latter did not seem very relevant at the time, but was to come in useful many years later when he directed the Egypt Exploration Society's Nubian excavations at Qasr Ibrim. In 1943 Plumley began his first Coptic studies with Jaroslav Černý, the man who was to become the third Edwards Professor, and we shall encounter him again as a student at UCL. At Glanville's suggestion and with his encouragement, Plumley wrote his *Introductory Coptic Grammar* (1948), and it was he who was appointed Professor in Cambridge on the sudden death of his mentor in 1957, a post he held for twenty years.

I. E. S. Edwards, now the doyen of British Egyptology, is the author of one of the most famous and most often reprinted and translated books in the discipline, *The Pyramids of Egypt* (1947). An Arabic and Hebrew scholar by training, Edwards took Glanville's classes for the first two terms of 1934, walking up the road from the British Museum three mornings a week. He subsequently read Late Egyptian texts with the professor after work, either at the College or at Highgate. The two friends began an ambitious plan to compose a handbook on Late Egyptian syntax based on the Chester Beatty Papyri. Alas, this never progressed very far.

C. J. C. (John) Bennett studied at the same time, having already taken part in John D. S. Pendlebury's El-Amarna excavations for the Egypt Exploration Society. He is remembered as having been a cripple who had to walk with crutches, and who was permanently residing with his mother in a distinguished hotel. He had never received a formal schooling, not knowing any French or German. Therefore, he was not allowed to sit any examinations. However, he much impressed one of the German students as being a 'real English gentleman'. Bennett later became a schoolmaster at Colchester and contributed to the *Journal of Egyptian Archaeology* from 1939 till 1967. His most important article dealt with the growth of the Middle Kingdom offering formula. He died in 1977.

Veronica Seton-Williams too began her studies in 1934. Although registered for the full Diploma in Egyptology, she later changed to that in Archaeology. As a field archaeologist of repute, she worked with Petrie in Palestine, on her own in Syria and Asia Minor, and later directed the Tell el-Farain (Buto) excavations in the Nile Delta for the Egypt Exploration Society. For twenty-five years she lectured for the University of London, teaching the Egyptian and Mesopotamian options for the Extra-Mural Diploma in Archaeology.

Mention should also be made here of Miss Margaretta Kirby, who in 1934-35 registered at UCL as a part-time occasional student. She took courses in the Department of Archaeology in connection with her work for the University Extension Diploma in the History of Art, which she gained at the end of this session. Then, in the spring and summer terms of 1939, she did a part-time course in Egyptian with Glanville. This rather brief attendance in the Department seems hardly sufficient to explain why, on her death in 1962 at the age of only forty-three, she left the entire residue of her estate to UCL for the benefit of Egyptology (see page 82). Netherthless, the two terms clearly made a deep impression on this young woman, for the words of her will read: 'I make the above bequest in gratitude for facilities for happy studies and delightful contacts provided for me by the said College'.

The long connections of Mrs. Julia Samson (see Figure 26) with the Department go back to 1934, when, as Miss Lazarus, she arrived for her initial interview with Professor Glanville, and first entered the museum where she was to spend so much of her life. This significant experience she described to me as follows: 'One felt oneself hurtling down the millennia as one looked at the overcrowded cases, shelves, and corner cupboards, all packed with objects of wood, ivory, and coloured materials, some of them rather perilously perched from the obvious lack of space.' Her immediate reaction was: 'Heavens, what a lot of work there is to be done'. Soon she was given her first opportunity for active involvement in the daunting task.

On a visit to Brussels she had met the eminent Belgian Egyptologist Jean Capart, who told her to go back to UCL and display the Amarna material. Glanville took the injunction seriously and gave her *carte blanche* both to register and to display these artefacts. She recalls: 'What I got was an unevenly pitched wooden chair and a wobbly two-foot square card table in the museum, a book in which to carry on thousands of registrations, and an interest for life'. In his report to the Provost at the end of the 1936-37 session, Glanville specially noted the museum's obligation to her.

At the beginning of this session, Julia Lazarus had been one of the group of three taken by the professor to Egypt, where she had viewed the dig at El-Amarna at first hand, and Pendlebury had invited her to contribute a chapter to the final excavation report. It was Glanville who encouraged her still to take the Diploma in Egyptology, which she achieved in 1938. She was due to join the Department as a Museum Assistant at the outbreak of War. Instead, she entered the Civil Service, and it was not until her retirement twenty-seven years later in 1966, that she returned to her vital work on the Amarna collection (see page 84).

In addition to the objects Julia Samson had seen on her first glimpse of the museum, she soon realized that thousands more were packed away in cupboards and drawers, or even in the original cases straight from the digs. Petrie's daughter Ann once told Mrs. Samson that her father often said: 'I must find and publish, so others can do the work'. The need to organize and catalogue the collection was indeed to be Glanville's herculean task and concern from the day he took up Petrie's mantle.

Mary Chubb, one of Glanville's earliest friends and later his sister-in-law, recalls that some of the contexted archaeological materials were saved from oblivion due to the new incumbent's vigilance. Finding to his horror that many of the exhibits were unlabelled, without any kind of identification, he was just in time to prevail on Petrie, before he left England for good in the summer of 1934, to go round the museum with him and tell him all he could. Out of his prodigious memory, Petrie produced the origin and *locus* of many unlabelled items (some excavated over fifty

years previously), while Glanville rapidly wrote it all down. Much of the value of Petrie's collection was thus saved for posterity.

Elise Baumgärtel, in her publication *Petrie's Naqada Excavations. A Supplement* (1970), tells two anecdotes which confirm this early picture of the displays. She relates that nobody was allowed to touch the artefacts when Petrie was in charge. Margaret Murray once tried to clean a showcase when she thought the professor was well away. He returned earlier than she expected; the pots had to be put back, and the case was not cleaned. However, there is evidence that Petrie's restrictions were not that absolute, for in 1930 the big pottery case was emptied and dusted.

Dr. Baumgärtel also confirms that before Petrie left he had been asked to identify the objects. But she says that he marked them and had progressed no further than the pots on exhibition. (This tends to confirm the story, still current in the museum, that Petrie, using a piece of blue chalk, his favourite writing material, himself rushed around labelling the ceramics on this occasion. Surviving notations on some of the vessels and other objects add credence to this account. They are by no means all to be trusted, as Petrie was by now an old man and even his memory was failing.) She then continues:

> ... He had his own method for this; he hung over the edges of the pots small strips of paper, about 1 cm. by 2 cm., on which provenance, and, in the case of the Predynastic wares, Sequence Dates were stated. This was not a very secure way of marking. The vibration caused by a person walking past the cases caused some slips to fall off; when a case was opened, which needed some effort as the doors were warped, most of them fluttered down.

It was Glanville himself who began the systematic registration of the Petrie Collection, carried out in new minute-books. He used the numbers as far as UC.410 for the Amarna material, Julia Samson then continuing. Elise Baumgärtel and Käthe Bosse also took their share in the cataloguing.

In 1935 Glanville saw to it that, following a former suggestion of Petrie, the collection of weights was divided between the College and the Science Museum, London, the latter receiving its share on a permanent loan basis.

In that year he re-studied this topic, Petrie's pet subject, on which he lectured to the Royal Institution, stressing the commercial and everyday use of weights and balances in Dynastic Egypt.

In the same year it was decided that one case with some of the finer objects should be placed in the Exhibition Room for a year. The idea was that visitors to the College could view both these artefacts and a specimen of the carefully designed new 'pyramid' cases, and hopefully potential donors would thus be attracted. Not knowing the full background, Petrie in Jerusalem was horrified by the idea, and in May 1936 he wrote to the Provost to make plain his feelings about 'this flimsy idea' for display on a pretty-pretty basis. Stating that his collections had been made to show continuity of development in each subject, he continued: 'To remove all attractive specimens from a series is to deter possible students; rather the attractions should be bright spots which draw admirers to learn the meaning of them'. Under his misapprehension, that it was intended to rehouse the whole collection in such a manner, he said: 'The sense and not the show of things is the proper work of a University'. The Provost hastily wrote back to reassure him.

Glanville was also interested in the museum world in general. In 1936 the College Committee appointed him as the representative of UCL at the Museums Association's Forty-seventh Annual Conference, held at Leeds. In the spring term of 1938 he arranged two lectures for his students on 'The Use of Museums', to be given by staff of the Science Museum and the Natural History Museum.

Besides all this new activity on the collection, the passing visitors would also have encountered two people who were legacies from the Petrie era. One was Miss May Bonar (later Lady Thornton), the Assistant Secretary of the British School of Archaeology in Egypt, who had a desk in the museum, at which she was 'typing permanently'. She had previously always answered the telephone there, for the old professor had been somewhat frightened of this modern contraption!

Also present was Mr. F. Bolding, the general factotum of the Department. Listed under the heading 'College Servant', he had entered the employment of UCL in 1921. By 1933 he was fifty-three years of age and an assistant beadle (entitled to wear only a short, as opposed to a long coat). He worked in the Egyptology Department every morning from 9 a.m. to 12 noon, spending the remainder of his day until 9 p.m., as a general beadle elsewhere. For his fifty-five hour working week his wages amounted to fifty-eight shillings. With twelve years service, Mr. Bolding was entitled to a fortnight's holiday allowance. He is remembered by contemporary students as spending his time in running the museum laboratory, until Miss Lafleur took charge of it. This man of many talents may stand in this publication as a representative of all the College beadles who for some time served in the museum and who, each in his own way, have left an indelible mark on the Department. Mr. Bolding himself disappears from view with the outbreak of War; at its end he was too old to return to his post.

By 1939 Glanville had spent £1300 of the Egyptology Fund on new museum cases, two of which were put to immediate use for the display in the Exhibition Room, and for the key pieces in the Amarna collection. He was now in a position to report on the needs of his Department, which he did in a memorandum, addressed to the Provost. The author began by stating that, contrary to what he had thought, it appeared that the bulk of the collection was *bought* by Petrie during the excavations. This made the work of rearrangement, in order to produce an accessible and intelligible exhibition, a larger task than had been foreseen. He estimated that it would require a capital grant of roughly £4500 to execute the plans he had in mind. He stressed that it was a task that surpassed the possibilities of the Department. Therefore he advised the appointment of temporary curatorial assistance, as well as the acquisition of new cases and fittings.

As regards the teaching side of the Department, Glanville stated that the staff was inadequate. From the inception of the chair, the philological courses were always provided by persons other than the professor (he mentions Griffith, Crum, and Thompson). Lately, the field covered by Egyptology had been further extended. In the other universities that taught the subject, namely Oxford and Liverpool, instruction was primarily linguistic, and there the professor had no responsibility for a museum. In UCL he had to cover the entire field, philology and archaeology. His request was, therefore, that the College should provide him with a regular full-time academic assistant.

In an additional letter to the Provost,

Glanville explained that the sum of £4500 was simply for cases and fittings, and did not include the cost of extra museum assistance. He estimated the time needed for the redisplay at five years; the actual registration would take far longer (it is indeed still continuing). In a second letter, Glanville reduced the total to a little over £3000. He understood that in the next few years this could not be granted, but saw a possibility of making an arrangement with the old cases. The work on registration, however, should proceed. He also mentions that, following the imminent departure of Miss Mackenzie at the end of the session, he wanted a shorthand-typist at £2 10s. a week. With the money saved in this way, an honorarium of £100 per annum could support a full-time research assistant in the museum. The two proposals were agreed by the College Committee, but, alas, the War was to intervene, and by the end of the hostilities, inflation had taken its toll.

The students who were then in the Department of Egyptology, now regard the thirties in retrospect as a totally different world. All agree that they were overshadowed by the gathering war clouds, without knowing the precise moment when they would eventually burst. This blocked out any future and led to a feeling of impermanence. Plans could not be made, and it was a case of living solely for the present in a bright, brittle, and essentially ephemeral period. This goes a long way to explaining their fond memories of the insular, cosy, and happy nature of the Department during that era. Even though, with the rise of Hitler, the British Press became more and more anti-Nazi, those students from Germany who were studying Egyptology experienced no animosity from any of their contemporaries, or indeed on any personal level. This has left them with a lasting sympathy for the English character. The issues of the *University College Magazine* produced during the decade confirm the impression that the students were fully aware of the threat which Fascism posed to world order. But, according to one of the pre-war pupils in the Department, they felt themselves to be at the bottom of the ladder, in a position where they could do nothing. This did not stop them from anticipating the inferno which was about to be unleashed.

Chapter Five

The War and its Aftermath
1939~1946

The attic location of the Department of Egyptology, nestling as it did to the south of the great Dome, meant that it would be a prime sufferer from air-attacks. The Head of Department was well aware of its potential vulnerability in the event of hostilities. His fears were well-founded, for the Second World War was to cause more damage to UCL than to any other British university or college.

Early in 1938, if not before, Glanville had requested that space be reserved in the College 'cellars' for antiquities from the 'Egyptological museum'. Two repositories beneath the South Cloisters were allotted, which were sufficient to take the bulk of the objects he wished to remove, with the exception of a small number of unique or very valuable pieces which he proposed to move out of London. Permission was later obtained from his friend Captain E. George Spencer-Churchill for these to be stored at his home: Northwick Park, near Blockley, in Gloucestershire (Figure 12). In September of that year, in the days leading up to the Munich crisis, these selected objects were hastily packed, having first been removed from their marble mounts if necessary. At the end of March the following year, seven specially made cases containing these 'best and most fragile and important items in the Collection' were dispatched to Northwick Park, one more following shortly afterwards. In this matter, Glanville acted entirely on his own initiative, without waiting to obtain the College Committee's permission. The owner of the property was also storing objects for both the British Museum and the Ashmolean Museum. As the house itself contained a valuable collection of pictures and antiquities, it had long been rendered burglar-proof, and the basement had now been especially prepared to receive the evacuated treasures. The eight clearly labelled UCL packing-cases were laid 'on trestles in a cellar which has been thoroughly dried out'.

In May 1939 Glanville wrote to the Provost, Sir Allen Mawer, informing him that he proposed to remove the remainder of the collection to the South Vaults. Stout raised platforms, about four feet from the ground, were needed in four of the bays here to house the loose pottery above possible flooding levels. The professor hired fifty tea-chests from Maple's, the furniture emporium, at a cost of half-a-crown each for the duration of the War, a considerably cheaper course than having new containers made. He also obtained the requisite packing materials. (In the long run well over twenty bales of wood-wool were used, but this was sometimes insufficient to prevent damage to the objects, as became apparent when certain cases were eventually unpacked.) If he himself were to be called up immediately, Miss Mackenzie, Dr. Baumgärtel and Miss Lafleur would superintend the removal.

The process then continued at intervals during that summer. In August, just before the outbreak of War, all the available students, as well as the staff, including the professor and Mr. Bolding, were deployed in carrying the enormous pottery collection down to the vaults. Both Margaret Drower and Julia Samson recall the circuitous and tiring trek. One would first walk down the tortuous spiral staircase connecting the Department with the Octagon, then to the ground floor, proceeding along the entire length of the South Cloisters, before making a final descent into the basement, where at last their loads were deposited on the raised platforms. Mr. Shiah is particularly remembered as carrying a huge Predynastic pot, almost as big as himself! But

12. *Northwick Park, Gloucestershire (above) and its wartime owner Captain E. G. Spencer-Churchill, with his collection of antiquities (left). (Courtesy of Mr. John Gill.)*

it was, they say, just this sheer physical activity that kept them sane in those incredibly tense days before the inevitable declaration of War. On the 5th September all the packing could stop: a total of one hundred and sixty cases (over three times the number Glanville had estimated in May) were stowed in both the South and Refectory Vaults. The antiquities now left in the Department were all housed in the drawers of the exhibition cases, with the exception of a small quantity of relatively unimportant items.

Meanwhile, the more valuable tomes from the Edwards Library had initially been stored, together with other College books, in the Cloisters. In April 1939 additional sand-bags and corrugated iron had been provided for their protection. Later on, these particular Egyptology books were sent, together with the manuscripts and rare books from the College Library, to Aberystwyth, one of UCL's evacuation centres. Here they were accommodated, for the duration of the War, in the solid rock cellars of the National Library of Wales. For the time being, the remainder of the Edwards Library (the proportion is completely unknown) seems to have been left *in situ.*

In October 1939 new entrants to UCL were refused and the various departments immediately scattered to nine far-flung locations. The Arts subjects, such as Classics, English, and German, were henceforth taught at Aberystwyth, but the small and understaffed Department of Egyptology was simply forced to close down. However, in January 1940, when the hostilities turned out provisionally to be a 'phoney war', Glanville requested that it be opened up again. This the Provost categorically refused: 'It is impossible to have any half way stage between the College being closed and the College being open'. In addition, there was no heating in the buildings, and the black-out regulations would naturally have presented a considerable problem given the Department's attic location.

In May of the same year, Glanville managed to secure the appointment of Elise Baumgärtel as a part-time Temporary Assistant. Sir Robert Mond, who had been subsidizing her for as long as the Edwards Professor could make use of her help, had died in 1938, and his widow now decided to terminate this arrangement. Moreover, Glanville had stated that 'her services would be the first I would ask the College to pay for out of whatever funds may be available for the Department of Egyptology'. The position was strictly for the duration of the War, and only if the College returned to London!

The relevant copy of the College Calendar still sets out the planned teaching scheme for the 1940-41 session. As Glanville had been called up, Dr. Baumgärtel would give Middle Egyptian, with the assistance of Margaret Drower, appointed as Lecturer in the Department for this year; the latter would also be responsible for the language course at the evening class. Miss Lafleur is listed as continuing her six lectures on restoration. In practice, however, none of this was ever carried out. The College had to be re-evacuated in October 1940. For the 1941-42 session no courses in Egyptology are any more mentioned, and from 1942 until 1946 only Glanville and Miss Lafleur are listed as members of staff. Dr. Baumgärtel's appointment had been terminated in June 1941.

The re-evacuation had been occasioned by the havoc generated on the night of the 18th September 1940, when the College was bombed for the first time in the air-raids of the London Blitz. The Great Hall and the Carey Foster Physics Laboratory were entirely destroyed. Irreparable loss was caused both to the North and the South (Arts) Wings and the Dome, aggravated by the incendiary bombs which fell a few days later. Due to its vulnerable top floor position, the Department of Egyptology suffered damage to its roof, windows, and doors. Fortunately, no direct harm was done to any of the remaining antiquities there, although rain was soon to cause considerable problems, for the Department's fabric had been left badly exposed to the elements.

Miss Lafleur immediately returned to the College to take charge of the removal, down to the vaults, of all the material left in the museum. As no boxes were available, the objects had to be placed in trays and drawers, which slowed down the process considerably. Even the heavy and cumbersome showcases were removed. Assisted only by College porters and occasionally by a former student able to give a little time, Violette Lafleur undertook long and arduous days until, at the end of December, the task was finally completed. The professor, who had been called up into the Royal Air Force, could merely look in from time to time, once offering her a lunch of 'oysters and porridge!'.

The College Library, especially the Science Library north of the Dome, had suffered most terribly in the air-raid, 100,000 books and pamphlets being destroyed. Many others were badly damaged by damp and rain, and had to be removed and dried out. Some volumes of the Edwards Library were also lost; at least, a record of 1948 mentions 'the considerable gaps, mostly caused by enemy action'. But the greater part, even those affected by water, was saved. It is reported that Egyptological works were amongst those soon removed to Stanstead Bury, near Ware, in Hertfordshire, where the College's administrative headquarters were established. The aim was to keep here a skeleton library of the most essential books, which would be the first to return at the end of the War. What happened with the bulk of the Egyptological volumes is not clear. Anyhow, they appear on the whole to have escaped destruction. The vicissitudes of the Petrie Collection were less fortunate and more prolonged.

On the 16th April 1941 the College was hit for the second time in another heavy attack. This time both the main building south of the Dome and the Dome itself were largely destroyed by fire from incendiary bombs. The now empty Egyptology De-

13. *The wartime destruction of the College, with the roofless and gutted Egyptology Department visible in the centre in a direct line with the Dome, April 1941. (Courtesy of the UCL Records Office.)*

partment was completely gutted. It is seen here in its sorry wartime state (Figure 13). Indeed, the entire superstructure above the vaults where the collection was stored was burnt out, largely because it took a considerable time before the fire engines could reach the building. Nonetheless, when Glanville inspected the antiquities the following day he found that no harm had come to them. Around this time insurance cover under the War Damages Act was arranged - the professor had valued the entire collection at £10,000!

However, after a short time, water used to extinguish the fire began to seep down into the vaults, dripping onto the exposed pottery and some cases, while others were almost flooded. It is particularly regrettable that a box containing precious Predynastic objects, was among those most seriously wetted. It had been one of the eight evacuated to Northwick Park, but was subsequently recalled at the express wish of Dr. Baumgärtel who wanted to photograph its contents. Arrangements were now made to remove all the material into undamaged basement rooms, where it could be unpacked, dried, treated when necessary, and then repacked.

Only at the end of July could this take place, there having been no labour available. The Egyptological staff was prevented by their wartime duties from taking part in any rescue operations, and it was only due to Miss Lafleur, who at this juncture was able and willing to give up her W.V.S. (Women's Voluntary Service) work and return to the College, that Petrie's great collection was saved from destruction. From then on she carried out a continuous salvage programme, with the assistance of College servants and, during part of the time, of professional packers. Often she had to carry on entirely single-handed, which cannot have been easy as she was a lady of diminutive stature with the most tiny hands. When not supervising the packing, she devoted all her energies to conservation, using a room allocated to her within one of the Physiology laboratories, in which task she continued to receive considerable support from Dr. Plenderleith and his staff

14. *Compton Wynyates, Warwickshire. (Courtesy of The Marquess of Northampton.)*

at the British Museum.

Glanville's high-level R.A.F. duties did not prevent him from somehow finding the opportunity to engage in a copious correspondence concerning the salvage of the collection. The plan was to repack the objects, either in the old dried-out or in new cases, for storage at Compton Wynyates (Figure 14). One of the properties of the sixth Marquess of Northampton at Tysoe in Warwickshire, it lies some five miles west of Banbury. It was then in use by the British Museum which, as we shall see below, was about to vacate this stately home.

An estimate was therefore obtained from the Pall Mall Deposit and Forwarding Company Limited, with its offices in London's Haymarket, for the provision of a hundred and fifty specially constructed eight cubic feet cases, plus two hundred crates for the pottery and larger pieces of stoneware. The basic problem, which was to cause repercussions later, was that the firm was unable to view the full contents of the various rooms in the vaults as 'they were full up to the doors'. They decided that a maximum of £400 would be needed for the cases, plus up to £40 for labour and time spent on packing, the basis of their high calculation being 'to charge cost plus a profit of twenty-five per cent on our actual outlay for time, cartage, material, etc.'. Even at this early stage, Glanville felt that the Pall Mall Co. had underestimated both the extent of the collection and the materials required to pack it all, and that the cost would therefore probably exceed the estimate. However, as he told the Provost, they were fortunate to find anybody who was willing to undertake the job, so they must accept whatever the cost, for: 'If anything happened to it which could have been prevented, we should have to shoulder a grave responsibility'. The main essential, he stressed, was to proceed with the packing as quickly as possible.

Because the Provost was not quite happy with the proposals, a delay occurred while a search went on for a lower estimate. Three months later Glanville had to tell Sir Allen Mawer that no other firm was prepared even to quote for the work, and that it was both useless to persevere and also dangerous to wait any longer. In January 1942, the College Committee, therefore, approved the sum of £500 for packing and transporting the Egyptology Collection, £200 of which had to come from the Department's own funds.

Meanwhile, searching for a safe shelter for his treasures, Glanville became engaged in a correspondence with the authorities of the British Museum. Its Director, Sir John Forsdyke, was approached with the request for floor space at Compton Wynyates. In this letter, Glanville evaluated the Petrie Colleciton as follows:

> ... except for some unique pieces, its greatest importance lies in its catholicity as a Teaching Collection, and it is, therefore, difficult to say that one lot of material is more valuable than another. I think any impartial Egyptologist will agree that in importance, the Collection is second only to that of the British Museum, taking priority even over the Ashmolean.

Having received permission to use this property, he wrote early in 1942 to E. S. G. (Stanley) Robinson, Keeper of Coins and Medals at the British Museum, who was based at Compton Wynyates. In addition to his inquiry about available accommodation, the Edwards Professor also asked about the provision of adequate heating: '... if not, we shall be moving out of the cellar into the frig [refrigerator] as we have some rough and ready heating at U.C., but quite inadequate protection against bombing'. Although reassurances were forthcoming about the temperature, Robinson's disappointing reply was that no space would be free until the British Museum began to move out.

The situation at the College had now become desperate. Just how serious, was made clear to Glanville in the 'very depressing report' sent to him by Miss Lafleur. She stated that the Petrie Collection occupied two ground floor rooms, two basement rooms and a passage, and five bays in the Refectory Vaults. Some of the sites had no heating at all, and the walls on the ground floor and in the basement were exuding moisture, with the result that the objects felt damp to the touch, as did the packed cases and crates. Temperatures should have been around 60° to 65° F. and the relative humidity 60%, but her extremely unfavourable readings had recorded temperatures as low as 40° F. with the RH as high as 84. This situation had already lasted for two and a half years, aggravated, since the autumn of 1941, by sulphuric acid fumes from the coke fires in the vaults.

Much damage had thus been caused. The stelae would literally have been reduced to powder, and the only option was to treat them *in situ*. The textiles, wooden objects, and papyri had all developed fungi, whilst some of the finest Predynastic pottery was flaking. Her restoration work on the moveable artefacts was also hampered, for the distilled water, used to free the bronzes from sodium chloride, had frozen in the vessels. Moreover, wooden items which had already been dried had again developed fungi with the approach of winter.

For the packing Miss Lafleur had had the part-time help of two of the College women ('They have cheerfully carried on throughout the winter under trying conditions') and of the College porters when required. Three professional packers from the Pall Mall Co. assisted that February of 1942 in the final stages, with the result that four hundred and fifty cases, including the tea-chests hired before the War, were now prepared for transport. The bulk of the pottery was ready, plus about three hundred stelae, kept in their original display cases (see page 19), reinforced with second-hand timber. Still to be tackled were the contents of five bays in the vaults and two basement rooms, plus about four hundred objects from Miss Lafleur's laboratory. She informed the Head of Department that for this task a further £500 would be required, while £230 of the original sum was still in hand.

No progress could be made with the packing until more money was available. The Provost was far from pleased at the increased charges, but Glanville, with his remarkable talent for dealing with tricky situations, wrote him a particularly skilful letter. Dated the 10th April 1942, this states that the Pall Mall Co. had been careful never to tie themselves down to a precise estimate, and had originally refused to undertake the job at all because of the impossibility of quoting accurately. 'I think we must sympathize with them there as even an experienced excavator at the end of a dig has to have his packing cases constructed as he packs; and in this case, with a large amount of the stuff, piled up in the vaults, it was quite impossible to see every individual piece and therefore to estimate accurately how much space would be required.' Half the work was now completed, but nothing could be said about the cost of packing the remainder until it was all spread out. Glanville stressed that the violent changes of temperature and humidity mentioned in Miss Lafleur's report would 'virtually mean that what was left behind would perish under existing conditions'. Then, in a masterful concluding stroke, he stated that even if one or two rooms in UCL could be made weatherproof, the objects would still need packing, and, moreover, these areas would be required when the College began to move back, with no other rooms fit to receive the Petrie material. The Provost was clearly won over, for early in May the College Committee resolved 'that expenditure up to £1000 on the packing and transport of the Egyptological Collection be authorized. It was hoped, however, that every effort would be made to keep the expenditure below this figure'.

At the same time, Glanville had been writing frequent letters to Robinson at Compton Wynyates, informing him that the ten tons of antiquities in their four hundred and fifty cases and crates were now ready to be sent in five van-loads. At least the same amount again was to come later. He estimated that 4,000 cubic feet of space was required, with as much again for the second batch. 'The stuff is suffering terribly in the College under present conditions and with our facilities for restoration we cannot hope to keep pace with the rate of deterioration.' The reply from the horrified Robinson was not encouraging: there was even no room at Compton Wynyates for all of the first load, because the unpacked Ethnography Collection of the British Museum was now moving in.

However, at long last, the removal date was set for the 27th April 1942 when, accompanied by Miss Lafleur, two van-loads containing one hundred and eighty cases left UCL. By May the full quota of four hundred and two boxes, representing more than half the entire Petrie Collection, was ensconced in Warwickshire. In addition to the pottery and the stelae mentioned above, the contents consisted of stone vases, scarabs, and three tins containing glass. The UCL material was placed by itself in the dining room where, according to Robinson: 'The packers made a marvellous stack nearly touching the ceiling'.

The packing back at UCL could not be resumed until July. Glanville had to write to the Ministry of Works and Buildings asking them to persuade the Timber Control to issue a special permit for the 2,000 square feet of Oregon pine required by the Pall Mall Co. for the construction of the remaining cases. In the event, this seems to have been not totally successful for, as will be seen, many simple wartime tea-chests had to be used.

In August, the Ministry of Works and Planning informed Miss Lafleur that Drayton House at Islip, near Kettering in Northamptonshire, was available for further storage. It had already been found satisfactory by the British Museum. Its owner, Colonel Stopford Sackville, had offered centrally heated accommodation in two large drawing rooms (one over forty feet in length), which could support a heavy floor load. He required no rent, but merely a contribution towards the heating and fire watching, which was eventually negotiated at only £1 per week, thus putting a considerable expense on the host.

In July 1943 the move to this property was successfully accomplished: over three hundred cases were transported in two van-loads. Their combined total weight of approximately fourteen tons duly ended up on Colonel Stopford Sackville's floors. Miss Lafleur had had to secure a permit for this removal by road. In her application she argued that rail transport was unsuitable, because of the danger of theft and of breakage, following rough handling by inexperienced railway porters. She mentioned that a large number of containers were second-hand Ministry of Food tea-chests, with the old markings still visible, and that some years before the War, the Egypt Exploration Society had lost a case of antiquities packed in an Oxo box and sent by rail. A month later she herself visited Drayton House, where she found conditions entirely satisfactory. The house was heated in winter; in order to keep a check on the temperatures she sent some thermometers.

As she progressed, the meticulous Miss

Lafleur had compiled a systematic 'Packing and Storage Register' which lists the contents of the eight hundred containers (some are simply tins), with a check list at the end compiled under provenance or type of object. The only antiquities which now remained at the College were either duplicates, unimportant stone fragments, or those items (textiles, leather, and metals) requiring restoration; all distributed between Foster Court and her Physiology laboratory. In addition, the three large and valuable Koptos reliefs (including that depicting Sesostris I and Min), were housed in her room. Their removal, entailing a separate van, would have been expensive, and the packers considered that a certain element of risk was involved.

It is indeed remarkable that, in spite of the narrow escape from complete destruction, no objects were seriously damaged. The only exceptions, noted by Glanville, were one tin containing Ptolemaic cartonnage, and twenty to thirty limestone stelae, all of which had been treated and were of varying value. Without doubt this was primarily due to the unstinting efforts of Violette Lafleur, to whom Glanville was the first to acknowledge his debt. At the end of December 1940 he had written to the Provost mentioning the fact that, shortly after the September bombing of UCL, Miss Lafleur had had her own London flat blitzed. Although she had lost most of her belongings and was left with no home of her own, she had nonetheless carried on with her work. He concluded: 'You will, I know, appreciate this devotion to the College, and I would be very grateful if you could spare the time to write to her a personal note of thanks. It will give her great pleasure'. This Sir Allen Mawer duly did:

My own experiences in September and October and frequent visits to the College since then made me realize very fully what strenuous effort on your part all this work must have meant - work carried through under most uncomfortable and at times really dangerous, conditions.

Following Sir Allen's sudden death in 1942, it was left to the third Provost, Dr. (later Sir) David Pye, to follow it up with a further letter of thanks in March 1943. Glanville, he told her, had given him an account of the measures taken to safeguard the collection,

awarding her the entire credit for the avoidance of all but a negligible amount of damage. This was entirely due to her willingness to devote all her time to the care and preservation of the antiquities. After its receipt, Glanville informed the Provost: 'I know how much she appreciates an occasional word of recognition by the College of her unstinted service, and she will be particularly pleased on receiving a note of this kind from you so soon after your taking charge'.

In fact, Dr. Pye seems to have kept Miss Lafleur very much in mind during the years ahead. In January 1945 he wrote again to thank her:

It must have been an uphill job, carried on very much in isolation and even in dangerous or at any rate somewhat alarming conditions and I cannot thank you enough for what you have done and will I hope continue to do. It is the kind of work that, lacking an enthusiast like yourself, could never have been done in wartime.

Then, in 1951 at a Fellows' Dinner, he responded to the toast 'The College' and referred to the Petrie Collection and her efforts during the War. The sixty or so Fellows applauded enthusiastically, and the speech was relayed to Miss Lafleur by letter. The Provost had expressed a desire that there would be a permanent record to her in the new museum. As this wish has regrettably not yet been fulfilled, it is hoped that the dedication of this Centenary volume will stand as a lasting tribute from her successors to the valiant and unselfish labours of Violette Constance Lafleur (Figure 15).

The new Provost had taken charge of a deserted and ruinous College in which 'there was hardly a square foot of glass'. An engineer by training, Dr. Pye was to nurse UCL through its extremely difficult move back to the blitzed buildings and the planning of their reconstruction. In 1943 he informed Glanville that his aim was to re-site Egyptology in its original location but, like so many schemes, these confident hopes were never to be realized in the post-war world.

By 1944 plans were afoot to reopen the College in the autumn. With this in mind, the Provost wrote that August to his friend Air Marshal Sir Douglas C. S. Evill concerning the release of 'Wing Commander S. R. K.

Glanville 76356'. He stated that, as the Department of Egyptology had been destroyed by enemy action, much work was now needed to get everything into order again before teaching could be resumed. Sir Douglas replied: 'Glanville is ably performing a very useful rôle on the Air Staff, and we should be sorry to lose him'.

Not surprisingly, Glanville's war service had been exceptionally distinguished. His quick grasp of any problem to which he turned his attention, coupled with his undoubted gift of leadership, had soon been appreciated in the R. A. F. Within a few months, he had risen to the rank of Wing Commander and was entrusted with the control of a department in the Air Ministry which supervised the training and equipment of the Allied Air Forces based in Britain. It was a difficult task which required not only administrative talent, but also the ability, on the one hand, to command the confidence of these strangers to British ways, and, on the other, the power of advocacy to press their claims with the High Command. Well-trusted and popular, Glanville was soon regarded by these servicemen as their champion. How well he acquitted himself of his charges, may be judged from the fact that he was awarded British, Czechoslovak, Dutch, and Yugoslav decorations.

Such honours left Glanville completely unaffected. His M. B. E. (Member of the Order of the British Empire) medal was once discovered by his secretary lying in the wastepaper basket in his office at UCL. On questioning him, she was informed that he did not know what else he should do with it! Indeed, his essential humility rendered him extremely reticent about his wartime achievements. One of his post-war students, Judith Walker (now Mrs. Hatton) once asked him if

15. *Studio portrait of Violette Lafleur at the age of twenty-one, 1919. (Courtesy of Mrs. Lucia Turner.)*

he had flown during the War. His reply was, only once, when he had clutched on tightly to the rip-cord of his parachute the whole time, only later discovering that what he was holding was not the rip-cord at all! He also told her that in the R. A. F. he had 'never had a clue what he was doing'. Not until our interview, getting on for fifty years later, had she any notion of the real nature and importance of his position! This also held true for other interviewees.

Glanville was released from the Air Ministry for a six-month period from December 1944. Then, on the 3rd May 1945, an official letter was dispatched to the College

49

stating that his release expired on the 14th June, when he would be recalled. However, a day later, the end of the War in the West was set in motion with the capitulation of the German Army in North-Western Europe. The Wing Commander could resume his professorship and begin to re-animate his Department, which opened again during the summer of 1945 in its allocated temporary quarters in the Foster Court building (see page 21-2). By July the College Committee could sanction the payment of the Departmental Grant, delayed because of the uncertainty about the moment when work would recommence.

The summer also saw the return of both the library and the collection. In June the volumes sent to Aberystwyth were returned, the Library Committee minutes expressly stating: 'a number of these are Egyptology books'. The temporary hosts of the antiquities were naturally anxious to bid farewell to their respective 'house guests' as soon as possible. Almost simultaneously they were pressing Glanville to remove the cases. By mid-June four hundred were back, the second half following at the beginning of July. Unfortunately, four of those stored at Compton Wynyates somehow went permanently astray. They were numbered tea-chests, three containing pottery and the fourth stone vases. For the time being, the Petrie Collection was deposited in the basements of Foster Court where, subject to damp and periodic flooding, it was to suffer even more vicissitudes before unpacking could finally begin six years later.

A series of fascinating letters survive, in both the UCL Records Office and the Egyptology Department's archives, which, in addition to recording the official thanks of the Provost and Glanville to the owners of the three properties, contain the often amusing replies from their recipients. For instance, Captain Spencer-Churchill, thanked by the Provost for storing the seven cases containing the choicest and most fragile objects at Northwick Park, wrote:

I am very glad to know that your seven cases survived their eclipse here with safety - which would not have been the case, had they remained where Hitler expected to find them. It is indeed pleasing to know how many of the large houses belonging to country gentlemen of England served really important purposes in saving the country or its

treasures during its greatest peril, and though England has condemned them all to rapid extinction, even those most keen on their destruction may admit it was lucky that there were still a few left.

Glanville had previously written to the Captain telling him that his charge 'was the only part of the Collection about which I had no worries during the war itself'. As it would be many years before a new museum was built, he told him something of his present plans:

Meanwhile I hope to fill about six exhibition cases for which I have enough space in our temporary quarters, and most of the objects that you have taken care of will be on show within the next few months.

The Marquess of Northampton, replying to the Provost's letter of thanks for the use of Compton Wynyates wrote:

It gives me great pleasure to think that my home in Warwickshire should have been of such important service during the War, though you may have heard that a practice bomb from one of our planes fell only a few hundred yards from the house!

Finally, Colonel Stopford Sackville, the owner of Drayton House, retured home from abroad to find that his famous and valuable picture collection, which had been removed to cramped quarters, to make way for the Petrie Museum material, was suffering from neglect. But within three weeks of writing to the College, he too was able to get rid of his well over three hundred 'charges' and to return to normality by rehanging his pictures and displaying his antique furniture in the two rooms they had once occupied.

Back in September 1944, the Edwards Professor had estimated what his needs would be in the Foster Court quarters. Most of the Department's old furniture had been salvaged, but not, unfortunately, the large mahogany table, his own personal property, which had been used in his room for seminars. A replacement for this was now needed. Further, he proposed that the largest room allotted to him be shared between the Edwards Library and the exhibition cases. Bookshelves were still required, as were wooden shelves, to be placed as fixtures round the walls of the room which would be used for unpacking the artefacts, and also in the laboratory. Gas and electricity points were required in the latter area, and, finally, a telephone was an urgent priority.

As far as staff was concerned, Glanville's essential needs were a secretary, as well as a beadle or 'lab. man' to replace Mr. Bolding, one who could help move heavy antiquities and also undertake their cleaning. Referring to his 1939 memorandum, he reminded the College Secretary of the former agreement to employ a cheaper secretary and a research assistant (see page 41). This appeared to constitute a problem, for not only was there a great shortage of able-bodied men, but, as he said: 'shorthand-typists at £2 10s. a week are now unprocurable, and very difficult to get at any other salary. All that we can hope for the moment is to secure one who has just passed through a secretarial training College and has not yet reached the age of eighteen'. Even so, the difference between the salary of the cheaper secretary and Miss Mackenzie's salary was not likely to be more than £75, as against the £100 estimated in 1939.

A vivacious and popular eighteen year old was eventually found: Miss Nonie Whitaker (now Mrs. Hamilton-Martin), who worked at the College from January 1945. She remembers on her salary of £13 a month to have been 'very short of money and always hungry in my "digs"'. In January 1946 she went to Ceylon and was replaced by Miss Jean Tudor-Pole (now Lady Carroll) who had been a student in the Department during the 1938-39 session. She was to hold the post of Departmental Assistant under three Edwards Professors, each totally different personalities, before she left UCL in the spring of 1953. Her last boss, Professor Emery, had jokingly told her that he could not possibly have a secretary called 'Lady Carroll' working for him (her husband was about to be knighted in the Coronation Honours List). She had been encouraged to attend some of the classes during her working day, and generally received help with her Egyptological studies. As a result, in the mid-fifties, she started to catalogue the scarabs in the collection.

In the autumn of 1945 the teaching could resume with the Department's first intake of post-war students. One of them was Judith Walker, quoted above (see page 49), who provides an eye-witness account of how they found themselves on the second floor of Foster Court, where Egyptology occupied five rooms at one end of the corridor. This passageway also housed several pots, while the Sesostris I relief was hanging on the wall, so that it could be directly seen when leaving the professor's office. A fairly small room contained the Edwards Library, open, from now onwards, only to those who had officially been issued with keys. It was full of books which exhibited no noticeable sign of damage. They could all be borrowed if desired. A couple of rickety tables and a few chairs stood in the centre, looking as if they had been there for centuries. The whole atmosphere was rather Spartan, if not chaotic. Also present was the mammoth cradle, once designed by Petrie for the Lepsius tomes. Next to this library came the professor's room (see Figure 17) and the secretary's office. There was also a lavatory, the installation of which, required by Glanville, had been regarded as somewhat excessive by the College Committee.

On the opposite side of the corridor, next to the long and narrow 'workroom' where the cases would be emptied, was Miss Lafleur's laboratory. It was extremely dark and crowded. In 1946 she again had 'the privilege of rehabilitating the remains of Jeremy Bentham' (see page 35-6 and Figure 11). Glanville's daughters, who were then teenagers, recall seeing her at this task. Earlier they had been treated to regular chemistry lessons on Saturday mornings, 'with the occasional fudge-making with her own sugar ration amidst the bunsen burners'. The students, however, tended to enter this room at their peril as the Honorary Museum Assistant was always involved in something extremely delicate which should not be interrupted. In these years she was conserving papyri, perhaps the most fragile part of the collection. It will be realized that no other objects, apart from those in the corridor, are mentioned; Glanville's plans for the six display cases in the library area were not to materialize during the few months before he resigned his chair. There seems to have been no particular pressure at this point to unpack the material. The only exception was the bead collection, probably for Mr. Shiah who was writing his doctoral dissertation on this subject (see page 37).

The teaching was carried out in the professor's room where he gave courses in Egyptian, History, and Art; self-evidently, he could no longer deal with the actual objects.

Miss Lafleur was able to resume her pre-war demonstrations on restoration, but was very much confined to her papyri. Dr. Baumgartel (she had by now dropped the *Umlaut*) no longer had any connections with the Department, mainly because Glanville did not get on well with her, and disapproved of her disinclination to undertake any warwork. However, in 1946 she gave a six-week lecture series on the 'Early Civilization of the Ancient East' in the Department of Anthropology, which, like Miss Drower's Near Eastern course, was attended by some of the Egyptology students.

In February 1946 a committee of six members, including the Provost, was set up 'to examine the question of the future teaching of Egyptology', and four months later the College Committee set aside £600 as a salary for a lecturer in the Department. The appointment, made the following year under Glanville's successor, would be of crucial importance for the subsequent history of the Petrie Collection.

The first post-war students were certainly not pattern pupils for they came, as will be seen, from various cultures and walks of life. Mostly in their mid-twenties, they tended to be older than the average intake. This implied that they did not feel like students, had no involvement in College activities, even rather priding themselves on their aloofness. It was indeed a continuation of the insular pre-war attitude, in the once again relaxed atmosphere of the Department, but one that was now combined with the general post-war feeling of relief, mixed with an element of euphoria. Of those who began their tuition in the autumn of 1945, three merit mention here.

Judith Walker (Mrs. Hatton) had became interested in Egyptology at an early age, largely because her grandmother's cousin was James Quibell (see page 7). When she was ten years old she had already read *Naqada and Ballas* (1895), which he wrote together with Petrie, and she grew up in a house where various antiquities from his excavations were displayed. Now aged twenty-five, she had been during the War the youngest censor in the Ministry of Information. It was following her year's recovery from tuberculosis that she had her initial interview with Glanville. She relates that this intrinsically kind man felt sorry for her and stretched the rules to admit her for her two years' study. After leaving UCL she would take a top secretarial job, working for the Editor of one of the national Sunday newspapers, earning the princely sum of £8 15s. a week, rather more than Miss Whitaker had received!

Cyril Spaull, a chartered civil engineer by profession, joined the evening classes at the moment they started up again. Here he studied Egyptian with Glanville. It was also in 1945 that he became a member of the Egypt Exploration Society Committee. He would remain on it for thirty-seven years, serving from 1951-1975 also as Honorary Librarian and Reviews Editor. Later on, he used to give occasional classes in Egyptian at Cambridge to help the students. Particularly interested in grammar, he helped Raymond Faulkner in preparing his translations of Egyptian funerary texts. As an Honorary Research Fellow of the Egyptology Department at UCL, he worked for many years on the unpublished hieratic papyri from Kahun housed in the Petrie Museum. These he had considerable success in deciphering, and his work will be included in a forthcoming publication by two young scholars. Unfortunately, his sudden death in 1989 meant that he was unable to complete the task. Cyril Spaull is remembered by us with affection as a gentle, kindly, and unassuming man.

Mustafa el-Amir was the first Egyptian student in the Department. He had previously studied at Cairo University, and worked at Memphis where he developed his interest in the mummification of the sacred Apis bulls buried in the Serapeum at Saqqara. From 1943-45 he had been Inspector of Antiquities at Thebes. Primarily a philologist, he followed Glanville to Cambridge in 1946 where he spent the next four years specializing in Demotic. His thesis, *A Family Archive from Thebes*, was published in 1959. Deeply devoted to his mentor, he regarded his years at UCL and at Cambridge as the culmination point of his life. Mustafa el-Amir subsequently became Professor at the Egyptian University of Khartoum, and later at Alexandria. Then he returned to Cairo where, before his death in 1974, as Professor of Egyptology he became Dean of the new Faculty of Archaeology.

It was early in 1946 that Glanville announced his intention to resign the Edwards Chair at the end of the session, much to the dismay of his students. He had been elected to the newly created Sir Herbert Thompson Chair of Egyptology at Cambridge. Founded specifically to encourage Demotic and Coptic studies, Glanville, as the leading Demotist in Britain and a past pupil and close friend of the founder, was the obvious choice. Ten hectic years were to follow in which, despite numerous other activities, he never slackened his attention both to his Cambridge students, and to the development of an Egyptological library in that University. As librarian and personal secretary, Miss Hazel Leeper, who would later marry the fifth Edwards Professor, was his constant support and help.

Glanville's activities were crowned by his election in 1954 to the post of Provost of King's College. Two years later, on the morning of the 26th April 1956, his fifty-sixth birthday, this unselfish man who had given far too liberally of his energies in the service of others, suffered a massive coronary attack and died instantly. Death alone had prevented him from attaining the office of Vice-Chancellor to which, in the normal course, he would have been elected in 1957.

In 1959 The Worshipful Company of Grocers, of which Glanville had been Warden and Master, commemorated his services to education by founding scholarships at his three colleges: Lincoln College Oxford, University College London, and King's College Cambridge. That at UCL was particularly designed for travel and fieldwork, enabling several students to gain their first practical experience in Egypt and the Sudan. After twice doubling the amount, the Grocers' Company substituted for the Stephen Glanville Memorial Scholarships an annual lecture at the Fitzwilliam Museum, Cambridge, where he had been Honorary Keeper of the Egyptian collections. This still continues, and the Glanville Lecture has, over the last sixteen years, become an increasingly popular event for scholar and layman alike.

As regards UCL, Stephen Glanville was able, in 1946, to hand over a viable organization to a successor whom he would help to choose, so that Petrie's Department could emerge once again Phoenix-like from the ashes and ravages of War.

Chapter Six

The Černý Interlude
1946~1951

In September 1945, Professor Stephen Glanville had drawn up a new memorandum on the staffing of his Department. It was prompted by his anticipation that, following the death of Sir Herbert Thompson in May of the previous year, his days at UCL were likely to be numbered.

The War, he stated, had created a situation vastly different from that on which his earlier report of 1939 had been based. Moreover, the death of two of the most gifted of the younger generation of scholars, Paul Smither and Alan Shorter (see page 23), made it less easy to find a successor should he himself leave UCL. Although it would be necessary to continue the archaeological tradition in the teaching, for the time being this was less pressing because, of necessity, any action for the rehabilitation of the Petrie Collection was now in abeyance.

With these factors in mind, Glanville discussed the immediate future of the Edwards Chair. 'On the assumption that a new Professor will have to be found to take up the Chair in the session 1946-47, I list below in alphabetical order six names which I think are bound to be mentioned when the Committee of the Professorial Board appointed to consider the future of the Chair meets. I doubt if any other names would be seriously discussed.' He then views his six possibilities in turn, not only evaluating their scholarship, but, in typical Glanville fashion, attempting to assess both their personalities and general cultural interests outside Egyptology.

Both Dr. Jaroslav Černý and Professor Henri Frankfort were foreigners. The former, a Czech national, had been led by his study of economic and social conditions into 'certain philological fields where he is acknowledged to be the best scholar working today'. Glanville further stated: 'He is without question one of our leading Egyptologists. He speaks and writes English, French, German, and Italian, as well as his own language; and is reputed to be an inspiring teacher. He has a sound knowledge of the classics. His manner is quiet, his personality attractive'.

The Dutchman Henri Frankfort (see pages 23 and 28), already short-listed for Petrie's vacated chair back in 1933, was at that moment Professor at Chicago. As an archaeologist of the entire Near East, he enjoyed an international reputation for his art-historical comparative studies of the region. 'He is a man of great vitality and a very inspiring teacher. He has great ability, wide knowledge and an attractive personality. Were he British and were the post to be filled a Chair of Near Eastern Archaeology, he would undoubtedly be, in my opinion, the best candidate available anywhere.' But Glanville doubted whether the Egyptologists would consider Frankfort as one of them!

The four Britons were Edwards, Emery, Fairman (subsequently Brunner Professor of Egyptology at Liverpool), and Faulkner. Regarding Edwards, 'a man of much charm and many interests', it was stated: 'He should in another five years be the obvious choice in this country for a Chair'. Glanville's words were to become prophetically true when in 1951 the Edwards Chair came up again for tenure (see page 70-1). Emery, who would then actually be elected to the professorship, was assessed as 'probably the best British excavator in Egypt today, with a remarkably varied experience of the country and a very sound understanding of Egyptian Archaeology'. He was also said to be 'a first-rate trainer of students in the field' and to have 'a thorough knowledge of museum-craft'. Faulkner (see page 22), 'a man of real worth, and well-liked by those who know him' would, Glanville felt, probably make a good teacher. Again these were predictive thoughts from the outgoing professor.

Of the two main candidates, Frankfort had the advantage of a previous close connection with Britain. He had a son with British nationality, who was being educated in the country, and he himself was a former student of the College. On the other hand, Černý had for several years collaborated with Gardiner, and 'there is no doubt that from the point of view of Egyptology as a whole, and in this country especially, it would be a matter of congratulation to have him here'. So Glanville reached the striking conclusion: 'Having in mind the inaccessibility of our collections, it would not be unreasonable to appoint a Professor whose bias was on the historical and linguistic side for a certain term of years, say five to seven, making it clear that the period would not be renewable'.

A matter of urgency stressed in the memorandum was that of a full-time lecturer to assist the professor. However, this had now to await the new appointee. In February 1946 Glanville added a postscript to the report, in which he definitely came down to a choice of Černý before Frankfort. 'Not only do I think Černý the best candidate available (if you are prepared to go outside this country) but his appointment would, I believe, facilitate the best solution to the archaeological problem. It would imply the appointment of an archaeologist to fill the additional teaching post in the department which has been promised.' It would then be possible for either the professor or his colleague to spend one term in Egypt every year. The ideal, Glanville felt, would be for Emery to be offered a readership, which would 'not only secure for the College a first rate archaeologist as a teacher, but would also assist in securing the continuation of Emery's excavations for the Egyptian Government at Saqqara - the most important archaeological work being done in Egypt today'. Frankfort, on the other hand, would need a philologist to assist him.

Jaroslav Černý was at this point forty-seven years of age. Even as a schoolboy in Pilsen, he had spent much of his leisure time studying Egyptology, and at the tender age of eight his hieroglyphs are said to have been as beautifully shaped as those of his prime. In 1915 he became a student of the Egyptologist František Lexa at the Charles University at Prague. Four years later, even before complet-

ing his studies, he was compelled to earn his living by working as a bank clerk in that city. His doctorate thus had to be written out of hours. It was on the history and constitution of the village at Deir el-Medina, a community of workmen on the West Bank of Thebes, who were responsible for building the famous groups of New Kingdom royal tombs, in both the Valley of the Kings and the Valley of the Queens. These artisans were to remain the principal interest of his life.

It was in 1925, on a visit to London, where he spent his summer holiday at the British Museum working on hieratic papyri, that he first met Dr. Alan Gardiner. The unlikely friendship between the wealthy Englishman and the struggling Czech was to determine the course of Jaroslav Černý's life. In both 1925 and 1926 his bank granted him three months leave of absence to undertake what would turn out to be the first of several missions at Deir el-Medina, assisting the French Institute of Archaeology in Cairo as their epigrapher. Then, in 1927, he was able to leave the bank with a two-year special scholarship from President Masaryk, in order to study the hieratic ostraca (pottery sherds and flakes of limestone) in the Cairo Museum. He prepared the official catalogue publication for the Service des Antiquités, having by now become pre-eminent in the reading of this difficult cursive script. When this was completed, Gardiner employed him in London from the autumn of 1934 for three months annually, to assist him in preparing a publication of his own ostraca collection. (Eventually published in 1957, *Hieratic Ostraca* deals principally with those in the Gardiner, Leipzig, and Petrie Collections.) The arrangement with Gardiner lasted until the outbreak of the Second World War. Černý also held from 1929 onwards the post of Privatdozent at the University of Prague, but this was hardly more than a part-time administrative position.

Unable to return to his native Czecho-slovakia after its occupation by Germany, he managed to make his way from Paris to Egypt, and eventually obtained an appointment at the Czech Legation in Cairo. In 1943 he was transferred to the London Legation, where he worked for the next eighteen months until the end of the War in Europe. Back in Prague he again took up his employment as Privatdozent.

In March 1946 a committee considering the future of Egyptology at UCL, did indeed agree that the choice lay between Černý and

Frankfort, and that it was desirable that the members should meet the former. A month later this had been arranged when Černý accepted Gardiner's invitation to come to London to discuss their joint work on the ostraca. (It should be emphasized that Gardiner was most anxious to have Černý permanently in London for this project.) After the meeting in May, Glanville started to press the matter, using as an argument that Černý 'was proposed by the Faculty of Philolosophy in the University of Prague as Professor in ordinary of Egyptology when the Chair is vacated next Autumn. This proposal still awaits the decision of the Ministry of Education'. However, it is doubtful whether such a post was actually available; Lexa, although over seventy by this time, would still retain his chair for more than a decade. Indeed, it is certain that Černý would have preferred a position in his native land, for at heart he belonged to Czechoslovakia for the whole of his life.

At the beginning of June, the Provost wrote to the Registrar of the University of London stating that the members of his committee had unanimously decided to put forward Černý. At their meeting they had found that: 'His English is extremely good and he has all the qualifications of a most agreeable member of the academic staff of the University'. He was in their opinion an outstanding Egyptologist, whose appointment would certainly be greeted with approval by the external experts. Matters had become much more complex since Petrie and Glanville were selected, for it was now the Senate which directly made an appointment to a chair on the recommendation of a Board of Advisors, with the addition of external experts. The latter were, in this case, Gardiner and Professor Gunn from Oxford.

On the 27th June the Provost could relay to Černý the decision, which had been agreed unanimously by correspondence alone, to appoint him to the Edwards Chair until he reached the retirement age of sixty. Černý's reply, dated the 8th July, states: 'I consider it as a great honour to be offered this post and shall be able to take up my duties from 1st October 1946'. He had been 'delighted' by his kind reception at UCL and expressed his gratitude to the Provost and his future colleagues for 'their consent to my entering the teaching staff of the College as well as for having arranged the matter with no delay'. His Faculty at Prague had 'taken notice of my leaving Prague and so far I have had no difficulties or embarrassment from that side'. He planned to arrive in London on the 9th September in order to have a week's handover period in the Department before Glanville went to Cambridge. Fortunately, a year's permit, obtained by the College from the Ministry of Labour in London, which was needed to enable Černý to leave his homeland, could be sent to him just in time to make this possible.

From a study of the original documents one gains the strong impression that Glanville and Gardiner had between them been instrumental in securing the appointment of a scholar who was a philologist, and a foreigner to boot. Somewhat surprisingly, five years later Gardiner put the onus back on UCL stating: 'Glanville and I would never have recommended Černý for the post in spite of his very considerable archaeological knowledge had it not been for the fact that at the time there was no other Egyptologist of distinction whom the authorities at University College were willing to accept'. Even though Černý was the only possible man, there were murmurs of discontent among the Petrie fraternity. Gerald Wainwright, a Petrie 'Pup' (see page 14), even wrote of his dissatisfaction and craved an interview with the Provost. A polite but firm refusal was sent. It was not so easy to put off Margaret Murray, who did not hesitate to visit Dr. Pye to vent her feelings and to tell him that Emery, an archaeologist in the true Petrie mode, should have been appointed. When all else failed the two together, as Wainwright was later to recount, resorted to a black magic ceremony to achieve their ends.

But against the new man himself no-one could ever level any criticisms, for Černý was one of those rare individuals, an absolute scholar who was totally devoted to his subject. His students once asked him how he spent his weekends and received the reply: 'I translate Coffin Texts in my pyjam[as]'. Helpful to everyone, he was loved by all who knew him. Shy and unassuming as he was, he could not have been more different from his predecessor. Committee meetings, especially his necessary participation on the Professorial Board, filled him with alarm. His favourite catch phrase: 'I am just a foreigner' underlined his basic fear of not being accepted. But such worries were groundless, for his students positively adored their kind, helpful, and erudite new professor.

His pupils all called him 'Father'. They would form a discreet guard of honour whenever he went out, for he was so short-sighted and so absent-minded, that they feared he was always in imminent danger of being run over when he crossed the road. 'Father' would also be included in their social activities. On one occasion they all clubbed together to take him to the Player's Theatre in the West End to hear Leonard Saxe and his old-time music band. Here they sang Victorian musicals, their professor sitting in rapt attention, avidly reading the programme, and attempting to sing along with his students. Once Judith Walker (see page 52) gave a party, borrowing a friend's home in Kensington for the purpose. She wrote a welcoming formula in hieroglyphs on the pavement outside the house, in order that the professor would be able to recognize it when he arrived. Unfortunately, he looked upset when he entered, as she had left out a necessary particle from the Egyptian. During the evening, however, he came up to his hostess with a beaming face, a glass in his hand, saying: 'Is alright, there is a Middle Egyptian text, without the particle'.

How considerate Černý was appears evident from the following event. Once he handed over a private language lesson, given to an elderly gentleman, who came up from the west country once a fortnight, to a student saying: 'Here, you have it'. As this paid £10 an hour, a staggering sum in those days, it meant a small fortune to the young man in question who was living on a £1 a week for food and a similar sum for his rent. The same individual also received unostentatious help with his tuition fees from the professor's own pocket. In later years, Černý would take the trouble to attend lectures by those who had been his ex-UCL pupils, and would always take them out for lunch if they happened to be in Oxford.

Černý was a true polyglot. There were few European languages which he could not read and, apart from Czech and English, he was able to converse in French, German, Italian, Arabic, Russian, and Serbo-Croat. But despite this exceptional command of languages, his students sometimes experienced problems feeling that 'his English was not quite with us'. Idioms, for example, could be difficult to unravel: a favourite expression of his was 'I cannot see a suitable tree', instead of 'I cannot see the wood for the trees'. It made it additionally difficult for those starting Egyptian, one of whom failed to grasp the

professor's pronunciation of 'relative form' for two years, before she plucked up the courage to question what obscure grammatical construction, a 'raty form' might be. The whole situation was also aggravated by the building work taking place opposite Foster Court at the time, (including that for the conversion of the new Petrie Museum from 1949 onwards). The noise from concrete mixers, pneumatic drills, and heavy girders being dropped, tended to make things even more difficult for the students. However, on a one-to-one basis, when carried away by his enthusiasm for his subject, Černý's English would often dramatically improve.

The strong Glanville leadership disappeared under his successor, but with Černý something unique and special soon emerged. This is best summed up in the words of his ex-pupil Dr. Iversen: 'as a human being he was in my opinion very exceptional, having an uncommon ability to create an atmosphere of simple unassuming humanity around him. Personally I loved him very dearly, and shall always remember him with gratitude'.

On the 27th May 1947, the new professor delivered his Inaugural Lecture (Figure 16), which was very well-attended. Not only was it the first to be published in the history of the Edwards Chair, but it is now internationally recognized as one of the most substantial ever given in the chronicles of Egyptology. Originally he intended to expand it into a book, but when he realized that he would not have the time to do so he decided to print it as it was presented, with the addition of one hundred and sixty-three notes. The booklet, entitled *Paper and Books in Ancient Egypt*, appeared as a UCL publication in 1952. The author described how the writing material was made, the thickness, width and height of papyrus sheets, and the number of them forming a roll, with information on how they were pasted together. He also dealt with the brushes, the ink, the scribe's palette, and the technical process of writing, as well as the illumination of manuscripts. Although differences are indicated between the material in various periods, no real development occurred, for it was perfect from the outset.

Three months before his Inaugural Lecture, in February 1947, Černý had written to the Provost concerning his nominee to fill the vacant lectureship. He was Anthony (Tony) Arkell, at that time Commissioner for Archaeology and Anthropology for the Sudan Gov-

UNIVERSITY COLLEGE LONDON

THE

PROFESSOR OF EGYPTOLOGY

(Dr. JAROSLAV ČERNÝ)

will deliver his

Inaugural Lecture

on

THURSDAY 29th MAY 1947

at 5 p.m.

Subject:

"PAPER AND BOOKS IN ANCIENT EGYPT"

Chairman:

THE PROVOST

Students of the University and others interested in the subject
are invited

EUGENICS THEATRE
Entrance—GOWER STREET, W.C.1

16. *Printed announcement of the Inaugural Lecture of Professor Černý, May 1947. (Courtesy of the UCL Records Office.)*

ernment. Černý had already approached Arkell informally and regarded him as the only competent candidate available. The main reason guiding his choice was that: 'Arkell is an unusually energetic person and a good organizer to whom, among others, the establishment, organization and development of the Khartoum Museum is due, and he would therefore be invaluable when the time comes to unpack and exhibit the extensive and valuable Egyptian Collection of the Department of Egyptology'.

Tony Arkell had won scholarships to both Bradfield and Queen's College, Oxford, but the First World War had interrupted his education. He served as a fighter pilot in the Royal Flying Corps, being awarded the Military Cross in 1918 for shooting down a German bomber by night over London. In 1920 he was appointed to the Sudan Political Service, first as Assistant District Commissioner for Darfur Province, later as District Commissioner at Kosti and Sennar. He became a well-liked and respected colonial administrator, inspiring deep loyalty and dedicated work from his subordinates. In 1928 he was made an M. B. E. for tracking down and abolishing an extensive and illegal slave trade between Ethiopia and the Sudan, a task which had eluded others. The victims were often little girls who believed the British would ill-treat or even eat them, and therefore detection was very difficult. Even so, he succeeded in arresting the dealers and created two villages to house the freed slaves. They called themselves the 'Sons of Arkell', and their descendants still revere his name.

From 1932-37 Arkell was Deputy Governor in Darfur, while in 1938 he became the first holder of the new post of Commissioner for Archaeology and Anthropology, with the task of setting up the Khartoum Museum. Returning to Oxford for a year to prepare himself for this work, he obtained both the Diploma in Anthropology and the Degree of B. Litt., with a thesis on the medieval history of Darfur. During the Second World War he served as Chief Transport Officer of the Sudan Government.

Although appointed in 1947, it was not until May of the following year that Arkell, now in his fiftieth year, could take up his post as Lecturer. Before leaving the Sudan he had to complete the reorganization of the infant Antiquities Service and the training of four Sudanese to take over his work. He also managed to rehouse and catalogue the antiquities of the Khartoum Museum. During the ensuing years, until 1953, he would continue to act as Archaeological Adviser to the Sudan Government, going there in the Spring Term of each session. It was in 1949 that he excavated the neolithic site of Shaheinab; together with his earlier work at mesolithic Early Khartoum, these digs were to ensure Arkell's reputation as the father of Sudanese prehistory. Material from both these excavations subsequently entered the Petrie Collection.

The relevant issues of the *College Calendar* during the Černý era list eight possible options in the Department for the Degree and Diploma courses, stating that: 'Tutorial or seminar classes will be arranged in the undermentioned subjects to meet the needs of students taking any of the courses'. There was: 'Art, Architecture, and small antiquities of Egypt', 'Religion', 'Old, Middle, and Late Egyptian, and Coptic', and 'History of Egyptian Civilization'. Miss Lafleur continued her six lectures, with practical demonstrations, on the restoration and preservation of antiquities. From 1949 she taught part of the Middle Egyptian course. Arkell, from his arrival in 1948, took over parts of the first seven options.

In practice, however, matters were rather different. The new professor had no ability to communicate with freshmen 'who knew as little as we did relative to him'. The situation is summed up by one of them as follows: 'As for Černý as a teacher, it may be questioned whether he were the ideal pedagogue'. Or, as an Oxford pupil of later years wrote to me: 'Černý could not be described as much of a teacher at undergraduate level, though he may have been better with adults attending an evening class, and as a D. Phil. supervisor was quite outstanding'. The beginners relate that their teaching was minimal; they had to press their professor into giving them elementary Egyptian and this one and a half hours weekly course was practically their sole instruction. If they asked him a question in class, he could not answer and simply went back to the beginning and started again. Therefore, they soon learnt not to ask him! He failed at their level, simply because he was operating at a much higher one himself. This was much regretted, as all acknowledged that their mentor really understood the mentality of the Ancient Egyptians. On the other hand, students who communicated with him on a one-to-one basis on a specific problem soon began to appreciate his 'rapier mind', which would immediately spring into action and provide instant answers to questions.

Indeed, Černý's nature led him to expand more willingly under the stimulus of new inquiry than it ever did in the course of routine teaching. The breadth of his knowledge was so extraordinary, encompassing as it did history, chronology, and religion, that one pupil in particular soon gave up using the Edwards Library and simply turned to the professor instead. She felt that he knew absolutely everything (never was she to meet anyone to compare with him here) and that there was no need to search further. For her it was 'very soothing' to find someone who knew so much, and was in addition so immensely helpful, enthusiastic, and inspiring.

There is a vague recollection of the class on religion, for in these years Černý was preparing his work *Egyptian Religion* (1952), which would be described by Gardiner as a *tour de force*. The rest of the time the undergraduates were simply left to their own devices, being expected to read up on archaeology themselves, for they had to write a special subject dissertation as part of the examination. They were also required before they had even started to acquire the rudiments of German.

It is remembered that Gardiner, regarded as the *éminence grise* of the Department, was around a great deal at the time. Sir Alan (he was knighted in 1948), decided that he would sit in on some of Černý's text-reading classes, which made the professor just as nervous as his students. At one point Gardiner came up with the suggestion: 'Jaro, make them stand up one by one and write it [the hieroglyphs] on the blackboard'. One hapless undergraduate, who could not draw, was thus forced to produce her quailchicks with their enormous stomachs for public inspection. Černý's good sense of humour immediately came to the fore: 'Ooh, he has had a big breakfast'. In fact, their teacher was tremendously particular about the formation of the signs; writing beautifully himself (Figure 17), he would try and instil the same standard into his pupils.

An evening class, teaching only language, is listed throughout these years. In practice, for reasons that will later become apparent, it only ran for four or five terms during 1947 and '48. The classes were held once a week, from 6 to 8 p.m., in the professor's room in Foster Court. Primarily for the convenience of people working during the day, they were much appreciated by the few who attended them. They found in Černý a marvellous and patient

17. *Jaroslav Černý teaching Egyptian in his room in Foster Court, with his secretary, Miss Jean Tudor-Pole, on the right, c. 1947. (Courtesy of Jean, Lady Carroll.)*

instructor. Some of the class would even follow him to Oxford in 1951 and continue on the same basis there.

One of these was Violet MacDermot, a junior hospital doctor. In 1947 she had been introduced to Dr. Margaret Murray who, on hearing that she wanted to learn Egyptian and Coptic, told her that she must go to UCL, and gave her an introduction to Professor Černý. But Dr. MacDermot's first instruction was to come from the former assistant professor herself, who taught her the rudiments of the languages, at informal sessions seated around the fire at her home. Violet MacDermot later took part in the Egypt Exploration Society's excavations at Qasr Ibrim in Nubia. From 1962-76 she acted as the medical officer there, also helping with the textiles and the small object photography. Her most important study is: *The Cult of the Seer in the Ancient Middle East. A Contribution to Current Research on Hallucinations drawn from Coptic and Other Texts* (1971). This monumental volume, followed by a supplement of another two hundred and fifty pages with Coptic quotations, fully reflects the high standards imparted to her under Černý's tuition. In 1992, our Centenary year, Dr. MacDermot has generously donated her important collection of Coptic books to the Edwards Library.

In the Department itself at this time there seem to have been nine students, rather less than the pre-war average of twenty-three. Under Černý the typical cosmopolitan flavour continued, there being a Greek Egyptian, two Poles, a Dane, and a Dutchman. Egyptology continued to enjoy a 'warm and friendly atmosphere', its pupils practically living there. Every day they would lunch together in 'The Blue Windmill', a Greek restaurant in Soho, then a cheap students' restaurant. Three of them merit mention.

Erik Iversen was the Danish student. Arriving in 1946, he followed Černý's daytime Coptic classes, in the company of J. M. Plumley (see page 38). The two men remember having to translate from English into Coptic, 'rather hard but very instructive'. Iversen also attended the Late Egyptian course, where Černý taught directly from Deir el-Medina ostraca, and the more informal text-reading sessions in which Gardiner took part. Iversen is particularly known for his studies on lexicographical matters as well as on the canon of proportion in Egyptian art, his two volumes on obelisks, and his fine book on the history of the hieroglyphs until their decipherment by Champollion. In these works Dr. Iversen shows, apart from his extensive Egyptological knowledge, an uncommon acquaintance with Classical, Renaissance, and later European sources.

Diana Kirkbride (now Mrs. Helbæk) also started in 1946, having been taken on by Černý as a diploma student despite her lack of formal qualifications. As the possibilities at UCL were purely philological, she gained additional archaeological knowledge at the Institute of Archaeology with Max Mallowan and Kathleen Kenyon. She also received conservation training there, which was of immediate use, for, after replacing Jean Tudor-Pole (see page 51) for a short time as secretary, she was appointed in 1950 to the post of Departmental Assistant. Her brief was to help Arkell to unpack the Petrie Collection and 'to assist in the repair and restoration'. On leaving the College in 1952, she became a full-time archaeologist in Jordan and Iraq, ending up as Director of the British Institute in Baghdad. She regards as her most important achievements the reconstruction of the Roman Theatre at Jerash, and the excavation at Petra. Married to a Danish archaeologist, she has been living in Denmark since 1965.

James Mellaart, a Dutchman, arrived in London in 1947. Previously he had followed the language classes of the renowned philologist Adriaan de Buck in Leiden. He came to London to study Egyptian archaeology, but there appeared to be no teacher for this subject. It also turned out, but only after a year, that he needed an undergraduate degree which he did not yet possess. During his preparations for this, an easy matter since for the compulsory languages he could choose Dutch, as well as Greek which he knew well from his Gymnasium education, he had plenty of time to write a postgraduate dissertation on the Sea Peoples. In 1951 he went to Turkey to try and find the origins of them, and thus began his archaeological career in that country, culminating in his excavations at Çatal Hüyük, where he discovered the remains of a new civilization. In 1964 a Lectureship in Anatolian Archaeology was created for him at the Institute of Archaeology, a post from which he eventually retired in 1991.

Unfortunately, Černý was dogged by ill health during a great deal of his time at UCL, which could not but affect his teaching duties. As early as 1946 he asked for leave of absence for the last week of the autumn term to consult his specialist in Prague about his stomach

trouble. Then, in August 1949, he entered University College Hospital with a rare skin complaint. He would remain there for ten weeks, bandaged up like a mummy. His morale in these circumstances was quite remarkable: according to Dr. Edwards, he never once complained.

In the spring term of 1950, leave of absence was granted to the Edwards Professor to work for the French Institute of Archaeology at Cairo on ostraca found at Deir el-Medina during the previous season. As in 1934, when Glanville visited Egypt, once again Mr. I. E. S. Edwards from the British Museum stepped into the breach. He gave one class a week on Egyptian archaeology and another in reading texts. His lecture series on the pyramids is appreciatively remembered by several ex-students. Then, in the October of that year, Černý suffered a nervous breakdown, followed by a relapse in December which occasioned his absence for practically the entire 1950-51 session. It was James Mellaart who gave three hours Egyptian a week to the three new students, two of whom were David Dixon and Harry Stewart who we will encounter later on in our story. The former was taking the newly-instituted honours degree in Hebrew with Egyptian.

Early on in the Černý régime, the Edwards Library received a bequest of ninety-three Coptic books from the library of Walter Crum. In addition to strengthening this section, these works also filled in some of the gaps caused by the War. Further bequests to it came from Mr. Platt and Lady Robinson. Gardiner also presented some volumes. Additions to the Petrie Collection were received in 1946 from Sir Henry Wellcome's excavations at Jebel Moya in the Sudan, and two years later Guy Brunton gave material from his dig at Matmar, together with some purchased items. Predynastic pottery was presented by Lady Petrie, and three Archaic vessels by the Sudan Government. In 1950 the Edwards Professor purchased a few ushabtis; six years earlier Miss Dorothy Walker had given forty-five of these funerary statuettes, obtained by her late sister from Sir Flinders Petrie.

The bulk of the collection remained throughout these years in its storage in the Foster Court basements. Only the Middle Kingdom Kahun papyri were unpacked for Professor Černý in 1947. That June the Head of Department complained to the Provost that rain had again penetrated the depository following a heavy thunderstorm, leaving one or two of the cases standing in water. He urged that a safe and dry resting place be sought, if necessary outside UCL. 'I am worried at the thought of what might have happened to the antiquities during the last few years, and am also frightened at the idea that they should remain packed up and unexamined for another five years or so.'

As a result, a grant of £16,000 was awarded for the 'accommodation of the Flinders Petrie Collection'. The Planning Committee decided that the requirements of the Egyptology Department were first and foremost for the storage of its antiquities free from damp, and, secondly, to have room for teaching purposes. The idea for space within Foster Court itself having fallen through, some buildings north of the Euston Road, about to be leased by the College, were first viewed as a possible home.

Later, a new solution arose, involving one of the two Shoolbred's stables situated, oddly enough, on the first floor above the Malet Place boiler house. Two schemes were drawn up, of which, inevitably, the simpler and cheaper one was adopted. The more expensive option would have resulted in a large second floor museum with offices and a library below. The chosen plan involved the adaptation of an existing store. As at that time Archaeology occupied the next door stable, there would only be room for the collection, which was thus for the first time separated from the Department, thereby of necessity contravening the wishes of the foundress.

In 1949 adaptation work started, hence the noisy building works which caused so much disruption to the lectures, as told above. By the spring of 1951 the 'temporary accommodation' had been completed; the floor had been strengthened in order to bear the collective weight of the antiquities. On the 10th May the unpacking of the Petrie Collection could at last begin. A few at a time, the crates were first brought up from the basement, where they stood next to the lavatories, to a ground floor room, and then carried across Malet Place and moved up the dray-horse ramp. Each was checked off in Miss Lafleur's register, the date of the unpacking and the condition of the contents being systematically recorded by Arkell or Miss Kirkbride. Some cases were found to have been used as nesting places for rats, which had eaten the antiquities, but, apart from breakages, the presence of mould and

extensive salt damage from both damp and overheating, were the prime causes of concern.

Thirteen small showcases, some of them damaged during the War, were repaired to receive the best exhibits. Before this could happen, grilles had been fitted to the museum windows and all the entrances made as secure as possible. By now Arkell was stating that he 'would not be surprised' if the collection were worth nearer £100,000 than the £10,000 valuation given by Glanville a decade earlier.

During his tenure of the Edwards Chair, Černý was to experience at least three major concerns, apart from his health. Firstly, he lost his Czech nationality. The Oriental Institute in Prague had requested him to declare that he had never taken action against the People's Democratic Régime. Černý stated this, adding: 'I have, however, never taken part in political activities, and I am convinced that I can best serve my country by continuing to pursue my scientific work'. Yet, he refused to state that he was willing to co-operate with the Czech Government. Henceforth, he would remain stateless, preferring to be attached to Britain only by bonds of friendship and science.

A second worry which, because of his scrupulous nature, certainly aggravated his illness in October 1950, was the position of Arkell. The lecturer had been appointed on a salary of £600 per annum. The College Committee had doubted whether this was sufficient 'for a man of Mr. Arkell's experience and seniority'; it might appear as if it wished to obtain him cheaply simply because he was in receipt of a pension from his former employment. Černý was consulted, but he replied that Arkell was satisfied with the figure. He proposed a year's probation to be set before a revision. For some reason this never took place. It was the former colonial administrator himself who, with Černý's strong backing, wrote to the Provost in September 1950, explaining his difficulties of making ends meet as a widower with two young children, and asking the College Committee to consider a more appropriate salary for him. Steps were taken for Arkell's recognition as a Teacher of the University of London, which was achieved in July 1951. Fortunately, a salary increase to £1000 per annum could also be agreed.

The third and greatest problem, which caused Černý to seek once more admittance to the Maudsley Hospital in December 1950, was the moral conflict: should he accept the

18. *The wedding of Jaroslav Černý and Maňa Sargant at St. Pancras Registry Office. Mr. I. E. S. Edwards stands behind the groom, while Sir Alan Gardiner is next to the bride, 14th June 1951. (Courtesy of Miss Naomi Sargant.)*

professorship in Oxford that was offered to him. Following the death of Gunn early that year, a vacancy was created which Černý initially decided to refuse, as he did not want to leave UCL. No approach was made from Oxford during the summer other than Gardiner's informal one. He feared that a negative response from Černý might mean that the chair there would lapse, since there was no other suitable candidate available. The matter was re-opened in December when Černý was officially asked to accept the chair. His doctors advised that matters should be settled speedily for harm was being caused by the emotional stress. They, and several of his friends, felt that he should best stay in London, remaining in his accustomed way of life. At this point, the Provost decided to take matters in hand. After consulting Glanville, who argued that 'it would really be in Černý's best interests to go to Oxford', Dr. Pye went to see Černý in hospital. He told him how much they would miss him at UCL, but that he must go wherever he felt he would be able to do his best work and that 'he must not have the slightest feeling that if he went to Oxford he would in any degree be "letting the College down"'. The visit did Černý much good, both in showing him Dr. Pye's interest and goodwill, as by what he had actually said. Even the

final obstacle of Gardiner's attitude was overcome. Sir Alan had for some time sided with the claims of John Barns, since he thought that Gunn had wished to be succeeded by his former pupil. But a difference of opinion with Barns led him to change his mind. He visited Černý in hospital to tell him so.

So, Černý sent a letter of acceptance to Oxford, and resigned the Edwards Professorship from the 30th September 1951. He told the Provost:

You will, I know, understand with what regret I shall sever my connection with the College, in which I have spent five most happy years, and I am sure you will believe me when I say that the acceptance of the Oxford Chair when it was offered to me proved to me a most difficult decision.

Thus Jaroslav Černý left UCL. During the next fourteen years, until his retirement in 1965, real happiness would be granted to him, particularly since the 14th June 1951, just before he left the College. On that day, he married Maňa Sargant, at a quiet ceremony at which his two closest friends, Sir Alan Gardiner as best man, and Eiddon Edwards, were both present (Figure 18). After a reception at the Ritz, the couple went for their honeymoon to Italy (only a few ostraca this time!). A fellow Czech, his wife would be his constant companion and devoted helpmate, providing him with the love and attention he needed so much. So he enjoyed peaceful years, although the gradual loss of his eyesight was a source of sorrow. He died in 1970, five years after his retirement, at the age of seventy-two.

There can be no doubt that Černý made the correct decision to leave UCL and to take the purely philological chair at Oxford, both for himself, and for the future of the Edwards Chair. The latter could now revert to its archaeological tradition, which had been interrupted by this brief interlude.

Chapter Seven

The Petrie Centenary
1953

The UCL Records Office possesses a bulging file concerned with the 1953 Centenary, and only a cursory glance is sufficient to show that its success was primarily due to the unstinting efforts and voluminous correspondence of just one man. This was the fourth Provost, Dr. B. Ifor Evans (later Lord Evans of Hungershall), who held office from 1951-66. Indeed, it is due to him that such comprehensive records still exist, for in a letter to Glanville he wrote: 'I am anxious to have a record of the Centenary documents and place them in the Library as I think that they will be of great interest on future occasions'.

The centenary of Petrie's birth fell on the 3rd June 1953. The idea of celebrating the event had first been proposed by his widow two years earlier. As soon as Ifor Evans became Provost a committee was formed to deal with all the practical arrangements. This had its first meeting as early as December 1951. It was throughout chaired by the Provost, outside co-opted members being Mr. I. E. S. Edwards of the British Museum and Dr. D. B. Harden of the Ashmolean Museum.

Ifor Evans kept in close touch with Lady Petrie throughout. He was later to refer to her as 'one of the most gallant people that I have ever met.' The indomitable eighty-two year old lady had many bright ideas of her own as to how the event could best be celebrated and displayed a keen interest in all practical matters. For instance, she drew up her own guest list. Her wish for a memorial service at St. Paul's Cathedral or at Westminster Abbey could not be fulfilled because of the proximity of the date to that of the Coronation of Queen Elizabeth II on the 2nd June. Nor did her suggestion that Flinders Petrie's name be inscribed on one of the flagstones on the North aisle of Westminster Abbey ever materialize.

However, her desire for a blue memorial plaque to be placed on one of their Hampstead homes was indeed realized by the London County Council (L.C.C.). The address chosen was 5, Cannon Place, Petrie's last residence in England where the couple and their two children had lived for fifteen years. However, the procedure was not quite so simple. Lady Petrie had wanted the inscription to read: 'Sir Flinders Petrie, 1853-1942, Egyptologist, lived here. He raised Archaeology to a Science'. However, after much correspondence between the Provost, the L.C.C., and Lady Petrie, the latter sentence was dropped, being against general L.C.C. policy for such plaques. Perhaps this was just as well as the L.C.C.'s initial design had misspelt the word as 'Archaelogy'!

Once the date of the Coronation had been fixed, it was decided that it would be preferable to postpone the Centenary celebrations for a fortnight to the 17th June. Again it is typical of Ifor Evans that he should have taken the trouble to write to Lady Petrie on the 3rd June to tell her: 'Although we shall be celebrating the Centenary on 17th June, I can assure you that it is in the minds of many of us in the College that the real day is today'.

All the expenses had to be met out of the £200 allocated by the Finance Committee, and the aim throughout was to keep the cost of the proceedings as low as possible, consistent with the occasion. A programme for the day was drawn up to comprise an opening ceremony for the exhibition at the Petrie Museum; a tea; a Centenary lecture; and then a reception followed by a dinner. The £80 cost of printing a catalogue to the exhibition, to be written by A. J. Arkell, had to be taken out of the £200, together with all other printing costs, for example, the invitation cards and dinner menus

(Figure 19). Once the cost of the tea party was included, this left only £100 for the dinner. It had originally been planned to invite a hundred guests, and then at one point a reduction to no more than fifty was contemplated. In the event, seventy-nine people sat down to a dinner, the cost of which had been cut 'in the absence of royalty' to thirty shillings a head including wine. Yet, according to one of those present, it was 'really top class respecting fare, drinks, service and presentation'.

It was unanimously decided to invite Professor Glanville, at that moment Provost of King's College, Cambridge, to lecture on the life and work of Petrie. In his acceptance of the invitation Glanville wrote to Ifor Evans: 'Your invitation to me to deliver the lecture is virtually a royal command which I accept with deep appreciation, if not very gratefully'. The aim was originally to have it printed at the front of Arkell's exhibition catalogue, but Glanville was reluctant as he felt it would make poor reading, and, because he was going to be in Egypt until Easter 1953, it would have been impossible for him to have submitted his manuscript by March. As a result, the text still lies in its typewritten form in the archives of the Petrie Museum.

As far as the Petrie Collection was concerned, it was initially felt that the Centenary might be the ideal opportunity in which to appeal for public funds to relocate the Museum and Department from its temporary quarters in Malet Place to its original location on the top floor of the South Central Building, at that moment not yet rebuilt. However, this idea was soon dropped. Instead, all the concentration went into putting on a worthy exhibition of choice objects from the collection in the museum itself, together with

UNIVERSITY OF LONDON
UNIVERSITY COLLEGE

FLINDERS PETRIE
CENTENARY DINNER

Wednesday 17 June 1953

THE PROVOST WILL PRESIDE

MENU

Cream of Asparagus Soup

Fillet of Sole Hollandaise

Roast Surrey Capon

New Potatoes   Garden Peas

Peach Melba

Mushroom Savoury

Dessert   Petit Fours

Coffee

TOASTS

HER MAJESTY THE QUEEN

THE IMMORTAL MEMORY OF
SIR FLINDERS PETRIE

Professor W. B. Emery

REPLIES BY

Lady Flinders Petrie
Dr Margaret A. Murray

UNIVERSITY COLLEGE LONDON

The Provost
requests the honour of the company of

Lady Flinders Petrie

in College on Wednesday 17 June 1953
for the Celebration of the Centenary of the Birth of
WILLIAM MATTHEW FLINDERS PETRIE

RSVP by 15 May 1953, The Provost, University College London, Gower Street WC1
Informal Dress   [PTO

ORDER OF PROCEEDINGS

4.00 Opening of the Exhibition of the Flinders Petrie Collection of Egyptian Antiquities by Lady Flinders Petrie in the Museum of Egyptology (Entrance in Malet Place)
4.30 Reception and Tea in the Joint Staff Common Room
5.30 The Centenary Lecture by Professor S. R. K. Glanville, M.B.E., M.A., F.B.A., F.S.A., in the Anatomy Theatre
7.30 Dinner in the Upper Refectory; sherry in the Flaxman Gallery at 7.00

19. *The menu of the Centenary Dinner (above) and the invitation card addressed to Lady Petrie (below), June 1953. (Property of the Petrie Museum, UCL.)*

20. *Margaret Murray and Hilda Petrie at the Petrie Centenary, June 1953. (From* The Picture Post, *24.9.53.)*

an accompanying catalogue. From general College funds £400 was granted to arrange showcases on the staircase leading up to the first floor. Half this amount was spent in adapting the stairs, for it was at this point that the ramp for the dray-horses was broken-up. Unknowing visitors still ask us if this entrance was designed to resemble that of the grand gallery of the Great Pyramid! Additional lighting, heating, and wooden platforms or 'shelves' on which to stand the display cases on the stairs, had all to be provided. This adaptation for the exhibition was designed to be a permanent feature of the Department, as indeed it has been to the present day.

The other half of the £400 was taken up with the conversion of the old showcases from Sir Robert Mond's study, which had been in the possession of the Department since before the War. Arkell even managed to persuade the Provost to release a further £200 for additional trays needed for his museum cupboards.

At the same time other temporary exhibitions were being planned at the British Museum and the Ashmolean Museum. An exhibition of Petrie's Palestinian material, which formed the nucleus of the Institute of Archaeology's teaching collection, was to be on show in its quarters at St. John's Lodge, Regent's Park. The Manchester University Museum was to put on a special display of objects from Petrie's Kahun excavations; and there was also a commemorative exhibition at the Royal Ontario Museum, Toronto.

Advance publicity for the event was both extensive and impressive. Three-page press announcements regarding the Centenary celebrations were sent to the news editors of eighty-two newspapers and press agencies in London and the provinces; the United States; Canada; India and Pakistan; Australia and New Zealand; plus a number of religious publications. Professor Emery wrote a prominent article in *The Times* on the 8th June; and others appeared in the *Museums Journal* and *The Illustrated London News*. There was also a request that the Centenary Exhibition should be announced on posters in the London Underground in July, but whether it was granted is uncertain. On the 7th June, Margaret Murray and Glanville broadcast on the Third Programme, the latter giving a shortened version of his Centenary lecture which was then published in *The Listener*. But the real coup was a twenty minute television programme on the B.B.C. on Monday 8th, during which some of the treasures from the Petrie Collection were shown. They had been taken along to the studio by Arkell, who talked about each of them. The programme was introduced by Glyn Daniel and also featured Margaret Murray.

As Wednesday 17th June finally dawned the elaborate preparations neared completion. Unsightly areas in College had been newly painted or screened off, for instance, the ugly base of the statue of the Archangel Michael in the North Cloisters; windows and floors were cleaned, red carpets laid and new curtains hung. A hundred and thirty guests duly arrived, divided into 'A' or 'B' categories, the former being the eighty who were to attend the whole proceedings, and the latter those not invited to the opening ceremony or the dinner.

At 4 p.m. the guest-of-honour Lady Petrie, frail, white-haired and leaning on a stick opened the exhibition (Figure 20). She was accompanied by her two children, John and Ann Petrie, her daughter-in-law Anne, and small granddaughter Lisette. Her short speech deserves to be quoted in full:

Mr. Provost, and friends of Archaeology.

When Flinders delved, antiquities poured in day by day to be studied - you see many of the small ones here - and from month to month we had access to those found by villagers, in Upper Egypt. When he bought unique objects, and also any puzzling ones, it was to make sense of them; and so this Flinders Petrie Collection is made up of small but picked specimens. I was curator of them fifty years ago.

Please tell your friends about this Collection and in future send them to see it; they will be welcome here and this unpacked portion of the Collection well repays a visit. It is essentially a teaching collection, and arranged so that the spoken word and book knowledge may always be supplemented by actual specimens.

She then handed the Provost a cheque for £100 as the first contribution towards her brainchild: a Flinders Petrie Scholarship in field archaeology, which still exists (see page 74). When the envelope supposed to contain Lady Petrie's cheque was opened, it turned out that her laundry bill was inside! The cheque had remained in her handbag. Only a week later did she hand it over to Professor Emery.

The eighty visitors were able to see a display housed in thirteen cases, with drawers below, which had all survived the War, although scars from the incendiary bombs that had partially destroyed the College could be seen on one or two of the glass panels. Four table cases had been borrowed from the Wellcome Historical Medical Museum (Figure 21). The Mond showcases were in place down the stairs, together with two of the original big glass-fronted vitrines from the 1915 museum (which are still extant). When ascending the staircase, one was confronted at the top by the third de Laszlo portrait of Petrie, generously

21. *The Museum at the time of the Centenary Exhibition, 1953. (Property of the Petrie Museum, UCL.)*

67

loaned by his widow (see page 26). Along the walls of the main museum there were eighty cupboards with interchangeable trays completely full of objects. As Lady Petrie had hinted, only half the total number of tea-chests had by this stage been unpacked, so many prized artefacts, including a vast amount of pottery, were still inaccessible.

The exhibition was arranged chronologically to cover the Predynastic to Archaic Periods, but then became typological, corresponding with the original Petrie catalogue groups, such as toilet objects; stone vases; weights and measures; beads; tools and weapons; shabtis; terracottas, and many more. The Amarna material had its own display, and there was one case devoted to personal Petrie relics.

Arkell's new brief catalogue was handed out to each of the guests. The general public, for whom the exhibition was open from the 18th June to the 31st August, was expected to pay for a copy. The motivation for this is made clear in a memorandum sent by Miss W. Radley, the College Assistant Secretary, to the Provost:

> Do you agree that anyone else who wants to copy should purchase it for say 1/-? This is only one-third of what the booklet costs and the idea behind the charge is not so much that we shall reimburse ourselves but merely prevent people taking copies away casually without any real intention of reading them.

Although the exhibition remained open until 7 p.m. on this day, the guests were only there for under half an hour before they had to move to the newly opened Men's Staff Common Room where tea was served at 4.30 p.m. Here they drank and ate off the best bone china hired especially from Gardners at a cost of twenty-two shillings for a hundred and thirty plates, cups, and saucers. The normal canteen china had been considered inappropriate for the occasion!

At 5.30 p.m. Glanville gave his vivid lecture in the Anatomy Theatre. This was also open to the general public. The much acclaimed presentation divided Petrie's archaeological work into five periods, and discussed the merits of each of them. He also sung the praises of the collection as the best teaching tool in Egyptology as well as the high quality of the tuition of archaeology by the Department. It was followed by a short silent film taken of Petrie in the garden of the Hampstead house of de Laszlo, shot at the time he was sitting for his portrait. This made a deep impression on the audience, so many of whom had known the great man.

At 7 p.m. sherry was served in the Flaxman Gallery, followed by the dinner at 7.30 in the Upper Refectory (now called the Old Refectory) where the de Laszlo portrait showing Petrie holding a bronze statuette of the goddess Neith hung above the company. Dress was informal, evening dress having been considered impractical since there was nowhere at the College for the ladies to change, coupled with a feeling that if dinner was delayed to a later hour everyone would have been just too tired to enjoy the meal.

Seated at the tables were those who had been Petrie's friends, colleagues and students, including some famous personalities in the fields of both Egyptian and Near Eastern Archaeology: Gordon Childe; Kathleen Kenyon; Max Mallowan; Claire Préaux; Jacques Vandier; Mortimer Wheeler; John Wilson; and Yigael Yadin, to name but a few. Even the Prime Minister Winston Churchill had been invited, but had had to decline due to the pressure of work.

At the end of the meal two toasts were proposed: the first by the Provost was to the Queen and the second by Emery was to the immortal memory of Flinders Petrie. Replies followed by both Lady Petrie and Margaret Murray. The latter recalled the long hours both she and Lady Petrie had spent in dusting the tops of the display cases in the old museum which had a wooden floor that was never swept. Professor Ricardo Caminos, who was representing the Boston Museum of Fine Arts, remembers that the very short address by this nonagenarian was 'absolutely splendid both in matter and in manner, terse, pithy, eloquent, and delivered with a deeply felt warmth of feeling. Superb. There was a hush when she finished, and then thunders of applause'. After dinner soft drinks were served in two of the staff common rooms to conclude the proceedings.

Subsequent to the actual Centenary day there was a dinner for forty people (all men) held a week later at the Grocers' Hall in the City of London, Glanville being a Warden of the Grocers' Company at the time. It had been decided not to invite Lady Petrie for then other ladies would have had to be asked and, according to the organizers, there was simply no room for them. Perhaps that was just as well as, according to one of the guests, hardly anybody left in a sober state. Then, in the autumn of 1953, Emery and Arkell both gave hour long public lunchtime lectures at UCL in honour of Petrie.

It is fitting to conclude this chapter by quoting Dr. Ifor Evans once again. In January 1953 he had written to Lady Petrie: 'You will realize that conditions in the College are still far from normal and that we shall not therefore be able to meet this great occasion in the way in which we could have done under more normal circumstances'. Judging by the number of appreciative 'thank you' letters on file, few, if any, of the guests would have agreed. All honour had duly been paid by UCL to her first Edwards Professor.

Chapter Eight

Emery: The Tradition Resumed
1951~1970

Following his receipt of Černý's letter of resignation in May 1951, the Provost immediately sought Glanville's advice regarding the choice of a successor. Dr. Pye invited him to come and address the committee, newly set up to consider this matter. The former Edwards Professor categorically replied: 'my own belief is that the best appointment you could make in the circumstances would be W. B. Emery'.

At the relevant meeting Glanville expressed his view that if the College failed to appoint Emery it would then lose the tradition which Petrie had set up of teaching Egyptology in the field. Emery was 'the one man in this country who really could teach Egyptian Archaeology from an experience of thirty years excavation, and the one man who could easily take students out to Egypt, to excavate and use to the full the opportunity the Edwards Chair gave'. Although not a scholar in the literal sense, for he possessed no formal academic qualifications, let alone any university teaching experience, Emery, in Glanville's opinion, was, in fact, 'writing Egyptian history'. This 'rather out-of-the-way solution' would, he felt, 'do something rather important for Egyptology and enable the College to make a much more distinctive contribution to Egyptology than would be possible if any of the other candidates were appointed'. In this he was supported by most of his colleagues, including Sir Alan Gardiner, who, in a letter written a few days later, said of Emery: 'I am well aware of his defects as regards literacy, but his knowledge of objects would make him extremely useful to University College at the present juncture when the arrangement of Petrie's great collection is one of the most urgent tasks'.

Even so, the direct result of this meeting was that the committee's first choice fell on Mr. I. E. S. Edwards. It was decided that the Provost should approach him informally, to ascertain whether he would be prepared to consider an invitation to the chair. Glanville regarded such an appointment as 'fatal Egyptologically', for it would leave the British Museum without an Egyptologist. If Edwards replied in the negative, then Emery was to be invited to lunch with the committee as soon as possible. It was further agreed that the Provost should obtain the reaction of the Vice-Chancellor to any possible approach to Henri Frankfort, by now Director of the Warburg Institute and Professor of the History of Pre-Classical Antiquity in the University of London.

The Provost duly went to see Edwards, but not before he had unearthed the Trust Deed for the Edwards Chair and discovered to his considerable astonishment the clause: 'No person holding office in the British Museum shall be eligible to be elected to such a professorship'. Glanville was once again hastily appealed to, but could only reply that, although he had indeed been appointed straight from that institution, it was to fill a new readership created by the University. Lawyers were consulted, with the result that Dr. Pye was able to tell Edwards that the legal requirements of the Trust would be satisfied if the election were dated to take effect on the day following his resignation from the British Museum.

However, after carefully considering the proposition for several days, Edwards 'most reluctantly' declined the offer: 'In spite of the many advantages which the Chair would offer, I believe I can perhaps render a more useful service to Egyptology by remaining in my present appointment'. As Dr. Edwards himself told me, the determining factor was that he felt he could arrange for a Tutankhamun exhibition to come to the British Museum, 'which had long been a dream and ambition'. Twenty-one years later this historic display at last materialized when fifty prized exhibits were loaned by the Arab Republic of Egypt to commemorate the fiftieth anniversary of the discovery of the boy-king's tomb. Over a million and a half people flocked to see it, and even more were to read the instigator's best-selling catalogue: *Treasures of Tutankhamun* (1972).

Dr. Edwards further told me that he too was a staunch supporter of Emery, and could press his claims with his friend Eric Turner, UCL's Professor of Papyrology, who was on the Board of Advisors. The question of an approach to Frankfort was easily solved as the Vice-Chancellor did not want to see him move from his current position where he was doing fine work.

Thus it came about that the Board of Advisors unanimously recommended the appointment of the forty-eight year old Walter Bryan Emery (see Figure 24) as Edwards Professor of Egyptology in the University of London from the 1st October 1951 up to the retirement age of sixty.

It was an act of faith on the part of the University, for doubts had already been expressed by at least one of the new professor's future colleagues as to whether someone without academic qualifications would be able to maintain the necessary contacts with other departments. As early as 1948 his long-time ally Margaret Murray, who regarded him as an archaeologist without an equal, had alerted the Provost to this fact: 'It is true that he has no academic degree, nor had Petrie'. Dr. Pye had then told her that it would be 'very exceptional' for such a man to be selected, and that it was 'particularly interesting that Sir Flinders Petrie himself had no degree when appointed'. He promised to keep this in mind 'as a fact which should be brought out, perhaps at the appropriate moment'. One can now only speculate whether he did so and was thus able to influence the decision.

There were many other similarities between the new incumbent and his illustrious forerunner. Indeed, according to Glanville, the College had chosen in Emery, 'the nearest thing to Petrie that now exists'. It was only appropriate that the first professor's mantle should now have fallen on another self-made man who was also a born archaeologist with a genius for discovery. Margaret Murray once said: 'Petrie himself had a high opinion of Mr. Emery's work and knowledge'. In his turn, Emery had a great regard for his predecessor, although his especial hero seems to have been Petrie's student Rex Engelbach (see page 14), whose *Introduction to Egyptian Archaeology* (1946) he always carried with him. Emery bridged the gap between that older generation of fieldworkers and the younger ones, at a time when the grand tradition of British archaeology in Egypt was at a low ebb. By 1951 he had already made many spectacular discoveries.

Born in Liverpool, Walter Bryan had conceived a passion for Egyptology in his boyhood, fired by the romances of Rider Haggard. A brief apprenticeship to a firm of marine engineers provided him with the basis of his future skills as a draughtsman. After two years studying Egyptology at the University of Liverpool's Institute of Archaeology, he became an assistant on the Egypt Exploration Society's (E.E.S.) excavations of 1923-24 at El-Amarna. Here he first met Stephen Glanville, his fellow student, and the two young men immediately struck up a close, lifelong friendship. At the age of twenty-one, Emery was chosen by Sir Robert Mond to direct his work for Liverpool University in the tombs of the Theban nobles. In addition to finding some new ones, he restored that of Ramose in all its present day splendour. Exploring the desert behind Armant he made his first major discovery: the Bucheum, with the vast catacombs of the Buchis bulls and the divine cows who were their mothers. Thus he totally belied Howard Carter who had told Mond that 'young Emery' would not even find a dormouse in Armant!

As a result he was invited by the Egyptian Government to lead the Second Archaeological Survey of Nubia, provoked by the first raising of the Aswan Dam. From 1929 he spent five long seasons in the region, with Laurence Kirwan, an ex-UCL student (see page 24), as his assistant director. Sir Laurence recalls him as 'a dogged Lancastrian who, once an idea was fixed in his head, could not be shifted'. This trait was fully exhibited at Ballana and Qustul where he excavated the tumuli of the pagan (X-group) Nubian kings of the fourth and sixth centuries A.D. In 1935 he was appointed to direct work at North Saqqara where he discovered the tombs of the First Dynasty.

During the Second World War Emery took part in the actions of the Eighth Army in the Western Desert. Mentioned in Despatches and awarded the M.B.E., he left the army as Director of Military Intelligence with the honorary rank of Lieutenant-Colonel. In 1947 he accepted a post at the British Embassy in Cairo and rose to be its First Secretary. Even though he was employed by British Intelligence, and acted as head of the local branch of MI5, he was always regarded most favourably by the Egyptian Government.

Emery's diplomatic skills were of value when he arrived at UCL in 1951. His sincerity and straight-forwardness, coupled with a sense of humour and sociability, soon endeared him to his colleagues. The relationship developed and matured over the years, so that on his retirement nineteen years later they were to pay him the following tribute: '... it is because of his *bonhomie*, his love of good company, his modesty, and his resilient optimism in face of continual difficulties that he is best known and loved in the College'. His sudden death a year later therefore came as 'a terrible blow'. As the Secretary wrote to his widow: 'I don't think there was anyone, ever, who was so much loved as a colleague or respected for his work ... Very many people in the College, including myself, are feeling that we have lost a real friend'.

One of those was the fourth Provost, Lord Evans of Hungershall, whose arrival at UCL had coincided with that of Emery's. The two men quickly established a personal friendship, and the Provost and his wife stayed as a guest in the professor's dig houses in both Egypt and Nubia. Following his Christmas 1965 visit to Saqqara, Emery wrote to him: 'I really miss your company after I have written up my Day Book. Quite a gloom descended on the household after your departure'. Indeed, the Provost took a keen interest in the excavations, often encouraging the Edwards Professor to stay in the field as long as possible. With his contacts in high places, he was able to promote Emery's discoveries in every possible manner.

We have already witnessed Dr. Evans' efforts to make the Petrie Centenary in 1953 such a resounding success. He was to be Egyptology's constant champion throughout his years in office. Being well-aware of the value of the Petrie Collection, to him 'irreplaceable anywhere in the world', he deplored its poor accommodation: 'still housed where Messrs. Shoolbred's, when they had a store in

Tottenham Court Road, kept their horses'. In a letter written in 1962 to the scholar who was subsequently to become Emery's successor, Sir Ifor (he had been knighted in 1955) stated: 'I need not tell you anything about the Department, how much we admire it, and the hopes we associate with its future development'. Its consolidation and expansion over the past four decades has been due in no small measure to this initial staunch alliance.

When the committee put forward Emery's name for the Edwards Chair, it recognized that his election would not provide for any philological teaching. Thus it was that in October 1951 Raymond Faulkner (see page 22 and Figure 24) was appointed to give 'Assistance in Egyptology (Egyptian Language)' for four hours a week spread over two days. As early as June, Sir Alan Gardiner had suggested the name of his erstwhile assistant, to whom he referred as 'a thoroughly practical and competent scholar', in this capacity, should Emery be appointed. Faulkner, now fifty-seven years of age, had held no post since leaving Gardiner's employment in 1939, although after the War he had taken over the editorship of the *Journal of Egyptian Archaeology*, the mouthpiece of the E.E.S. As Černý, Glanville, and Emery were all in favour of this candidate, the Provost asked Gardiner to have a preliminary word with Faulkner. Sir Alan duly invited his former employee to tea, informed him of the project 'almost in the form of a definite offer', and then advised Dr. Pye that any appointment should be continued up to Faulkner's retirement, for 'it would in fact be very humiliating to him if he were engaged merely for a year or two and then replaced by a man of greater attainments'. Matters were soon officially arranged with Faulkner, who had been 'deeply interested' in the proposition, and Glanville was asked to decide on a suitable honorarium. Promoted to a part-time post in 1955 and an official lectureship a year later, Faulkner did indeed continue at UCL until his retirement, which had been extended well beyond the norm.

On the 28th February 1952 the new professor delivered his Inaugural Lecture entitled 'Saqqara and the Dynastic Race', which was published by UCL in the same year. Emery now requested permission, under the terms of his appointment, for leave of absence for the spring term of 1953 in order to resume his excavations at Saqqara, this time on behalf of the E.E.S. He was soon able to report to the Provost: 'It has been a most successful season with the discovery of a great royal tomb of the First Dynasty; all very appropriate for Petrie's centenary, for, as you know, this was his particular period'. In 1954 the professor resumed the Petrie tradition of taking postgraduate students from the Department into the field.

From 1957 onward, Emery took part in the widely publicized UNESCO International Salvage Campaign, to save as far as possible the Nubian monuments that were threatened by the construction of the Aswan High Dam. It was on his suggestions, as a member of the UNESCO Consultative Committee, that much of the archaeological side of the campaign was based. He himself excavated in this context the fortress of Buhen for the E.E.S. which necessitated his prolonged absence from the College year after year. Often he left in September, not returning before the end of April. This situation even continued when he returned to Saqqara in 1964, and was actually to last until the end of his tenure.

The statement in the College Calendar for the 1951-52 session that: 'The primary purpose of the Department is the promotion of research', accords with Emery's doubts as to the propriety of teaching Egyptology at undergraduate level. However, there were three ways in which the subject could be taken for a Bachelor of Arts Honours Degree. Combined with History, the Egyptology option covered the general history of Ancient Egypt down to the Saite Period with an in-depth study of one particular period. As part of an Anthropology degree, Egyptology formed a subsidiary subject. Finally, there was the new Hebrew with Egyptian Degree. The course in Egyptology for the Academic Diploma in Archaeology, normally extending over at least two sessions, was open to postgraduates and those 'who, though not graduates, have satisfied the Edwards Professor that they are qualified to profit by the course'. Its companion, the old Petrie régime Diploma in Egyptology, still continued alongside as a three-year introductory course.

In the fifties there were only a few students in the Department, on average no more than three or four on all courses in all years. Eight tutorial or seminar courses were offered: 'Art, Architecture and small antiquities'; 'Religion'; 'Old, Middle, and Late Egyptian'; 'Coptic'; and 'History (down to the Roman Conquest)'. The eighth was Miss Lafleur's six lectures on the restoration and preservation of antiquities, which had now been running since 1939. There were also 'Special Classes', seemingly a revamped Evening School, offering both junior and senior Egyptian, still termed, between brackets, 'Hieroglyphic'. The professor taught the non-language options; Faulkner the Old and Late Egyptian, and Miss Lafleur the Middle Egyptian. From the 1952-53 session Emery instituted a new course: 'Methods and practice in Egyptian Archaeology'. Following Miss Lafleur's departure in 1954, her restoration lessons were taken over by Arkell, who, in the next session, also become responsible for the small antiquities, while Emery's classes were now simply called 'Art and Architecture'.

In practice, however, Emery's long annual absences meant that he played a very restricted rôle in the Department's teaching, often only lecturing in the first half of the summer term. He shared Petrie's dislike of 'spoon-feeding' and, according to David Dixon, reading for the Hebrew with Egyptian Degree, it was really a case of asking the professor questions if assistance was required. Eric Uphill (see Figure 23), at present a lecturer for the Extra-Mural Department of the University of London, did attend Emery's Art, Achitecture and small antiquities course in 1954, as a preparation for joining the professor at Saqqara. He recalls the strong bias towards the Archaic Period in these museum-based classes, revolving as they did around the study of First Dynasty pottery, stone vases, and small objects. Arkell's courses were also held in the collection, and were primarily for the benefit of the first-year students. In addition, he lectured on his special subjects of Egyptian and Sudanese prehistory.

It was only Faulkner who gave regular classes, thereby making his unique contribution to the teaching of the essential language element. The experience of his UCL students with no dictionary in their lodgings and only a single copy of the great Berlin *Wörterbuch der Aegyptische Sprache* (1926-31) in the Edwards Library led him to prepare in these years a reliable and portable volume. The resulting *Concise Dictionary of Middle Egyptian* (1962), has become a daily companion to countless students all over the world. Indeed, it is doubtful whether any other work since Gardiner's *Egyptian Grammar* is so widely used.

Faulkner was a man of rather military aspect, with a staccato turn of speech. His sternly disciplined attitude to scholarship could sometimes overawe beginners, but his classes were always conducted with spontaneity and humour. A common experience was for the Edwards Library to be rocked by explosions of laughter emanating from the tiny windowless cell, called by him 'the Rabbit Hutch', where his classes were conducted. (Now the present Computer Room, it is still more commonly known by Faulkner's name.) Uphill, who took Coptic with him, recalls one particular occasion when their teacher's worm-eaten chair finally collapsed beneath him, and the great good humour in which he took the incident.

Faulkner's patience with students' errors and difficulties was coupled with his firm insistence on a good hieroglyphic hand. He displayed a never-failing interest in their questions and suggestions, appreciating their initiative. Every reading of an Egyptian text was to him an adventure, a constant and enthusiastic search for new interpretations. No wonder that his Head of Department referred to him as 'a teacher of international reputation'.

A few words should be devoted to two of the trust funds instituted at the beginning of the Emery era. The bequest of Francis Ll. Griffith (see page 30) had been applied from 1937 onwards towards the payment of the salary of the Edwards Professor. But in 1953 it was decided that the income should henceforth be held available for 'the encouragement of the study of Egyptology in the College'. Emery immediately spent the first £200 on equipment and furniture to improve the lecture facilities in the Edwards Library. The idea was to enable the arrangement of lectures and discussion groups, such as had been a common feature during Petrie's days. In this connection a start had already been made in rearranging and cataloguing the Department's large collection of lantern slides, disorganized during the War.

It will be remembered that at the 1953 Centenary Lady Petrie had presented a cheque for £100 to found a Flinders Petrie Scholarship in Field Archaeology. To this came also the assets of the British School of Archaeology in Egypt, which was wound up at the time of the Centenary, after the publication of two more Petrie catalogues (see page 19-20). Moreover, its copyrights were vested in the Department.

The income from this trust fund is used to provide scholarships, of which Arkell was the first recipient. As few conditions as possible were imposed, and it is open to candidates who are not students of the College. The Petrie Fund also contains sums not earmarked for scholarships, which over the years have been used for various Departmental projects.

By 1952 nearly half the eight hundred boxes housing the Petrie Collection had been unpacked, but the 'temporary museum' was now completely full. The remainder still languished in the damp basements. The ground floor room in Foster Court, used as a temporary resting place for the crates (see page 62), was now equipped with shelving, a prerequisite before any further unpacking could take place. This room began to function as an adjunct to the museum and even contained some vitrines filled with pottery.

The use of the Mond showcases placed on the staircase for the Petrie Centenary Exhibition enabled more objects to be displayed. The museum was already equipped with its *in situ* storage in the form of white cupboards placed around every vacant wall-space (see Figure 21). Arkell had obtained more trays for them as part of the Centenary expenditure (see page 66). They were his brainchild, for he had employed similar ones in the Khartoum Museum. At twenty-two inches square and very robust, they were made to human scale to enable the greatest load to be carried without strain in the most convenient fashion. The multiple-choice cardboard boxes, designed to fit neatly inside without loss of space, were also his idea. The whole system gave total interchangeability, for every drawer could fit in every position. More storage units were purchased subsequently to make up our present total of ninety-eight main cupboards, each housing a maximum of twenty trays, and seventy-six smaller ones taking seven of them. These invaluable units have stood the collection in good stead ever since, as few drawers are anything but full to overflowing.

In August 1953 a crucial event for the future of the museum occurred with the appointment of a full-time, permanent technician to replace Diana Kirkbride who had resigned the previous December. Arkell had visited London's Central School of Arts and Crafts with the plea for 'someone to come and restore the Petrie Collection'. Here he discovered E. Martin Burgess (Figure 22), in the third year of his silversmithing course, who responded to the call, and, after gaining his diplomas, began work. First, however, Arkell sent him to the Institute of Archaeology at Regent's Park for a two-month training.

Burgess recalls that he was expected to work from 8.30 a.m. to 6 p.m., the long hours meaning that for the next ten years he was forced to shop every day at lunchtime. Everything had to be done at the double: 'I ran two miles every lunch hour'. Arkell would arrive at 10.10 a.m. sharp, and leave equally promptly at 4.30 p.m., but on five days a week, and through the vacations, he would work solidly, never pausing except for a break of less than half an hour for lunch. Burgess describes his new boss as a marvellous person to work for, as he gave him constant and total support. He never gave an order, but would remark: 'Do you think we should do so and so, Martin?' They were to work well together over the next ten years and to share many happy moments.

In his turn, the twenty-one year old technician brought many advantages to his new job. He was extremely strong and was able to carry a heavy tray full of rocks simply by manoeuvring it onto his head, negotiating

a stepladder, and then depositing it in a top cupboard. His brief was to make sure that Arkell, who in 1953 had had to undergo a hernia operation after moving so many crates, kept firmly to his doctor's instructions and did not lift anything. By the time this enthusiastic recruit had been working a year the number of cases still to be unpacked had been reduced to about three hundred and fifty, most of which contained pottery and large stone objects.

The problem of the lack of space began to be tackled when, in November 1955, the College Committee decided that the Department of Archaeology would receive two lecture rooms in Foster Court in return for relinquishing their Malet Place stable to Egyptology. At the same time over £6000 was made available for thirty display units. The sum came from the bequest of Professor T. G. Hill who, on his death the previous year, had left his residuary estate to UCL 'for rebuilding the College after the War'. It was now

22. *View of the inscription cases with Mr. Martin Burgess,* c. *1961.* *(Property of the Petrie Museum, UCL.)*

proposed that: 'the showcases, replacing those lost in the main building as the result of bombing raids, might be regarded as falling within the objects of the bequest'. Emery was requested to place a commemorative plaque in the museum; actually, individual labels with the words 'T. G. Hill Bequest' were affixed to each of the pottery cases.

However, before the move could take place and before the new vitrines were even ordered, a serious fire broke out in Foster Court on the 1st March 1956. It started in the Department's second floor laboratory, which had been taken over by Martin Burgess when Miss Lafleur left the College. He describes how he arrived early that morning to find fire engines, crowds, and water cascading everywhere. 'With horror, I realized the seat of the fire was my laboratory.' Burgess had installed an electrolitic cleaning tank there, which he used for conserving metals. Here the conflagration had begun, as the current which fed it was 'not all that safe'. In addition, above the sink were rows of highly flammable chemicals, including tolulene, acetone, sulphuric and nitric acid.

No wonder that with its wooden floors, the damage to Foster Court was so extensive, and the incident was widely reported, and exaggerated, by the Press. The flames destroyed the English Department on the floor above and took the roof off Foster Court. Apart from Egyptology and English, emergency accommodation had to be found for Geography, the Faculty of Laws, and the Library. All the charred roof timbers having fallen in, the floor of Burgess' gutted laboratory was a foot deep in wet charcoal. His suitcase, containing his best clothes and records for taking home that weekend, was totally burnt. Of more importance for the history of the collection was the presence in the laboratory of the original pieces of the reconstructed Hathor bowl that he was working on at the time. Burgess described to me how Arkell, who was due to give a College lunchtime lecture that day, spent the time before and after in 'that wet, roofless, black room' on his hands and knees, sifting the charcoal for the missing fragments. He went off to his lecture totally black! However, all the pieces were located and could be cleaned successfully. Burgess then spent the next week sifting all the charcoal bit by bit in search of other objects, going over the room twice in both directions to make sure that nothing had been missed.

Unfortunately, a number of antiquities were severely damaged, the papyrus collection being the main victim, although, remarkably, no sheet was lost. They were stored next door to the laboratory, where Faulkner had been remounting some of them in his spare moments. It is a wonder that this room remained unharmed, although the water damage was considerable and all the papyri, most of which were simply mounted between cardboard, were soaked. Arkell telephoned the British Museum for emergency aid. Dr. Edwards described to me how, what he euphemistically called 'this useful salvage operation' got underway. He drove up to the College, loaded them into his car and took them back to the British Museum. He then summoned Dr. Plenderleith (see page 33), the Head of the Research Laboratories, and the two men hastened to the House of Commons where the Victoria Tower was 'stuffed' with Acts of Parliament, all wrapped in impregnated blotting paper. Having obtained a large roll of this material, they spread it over all the UCL documents so that they eventually dried out. It lasted several years before they returned to the College.

Burgess subsequently remounted some of the papyri between glass at the British Museum. This work was later continued by his successor Stephen Harris at the Institute of Archaeology, but when he left in 1965 only a quarter had been remounted. They were then placed in a specially constructed papyrus storage cupboard in the Petrie Museum. Further conservation is at present in progress. Looking back, it is no exaggeration to state that, without the help of the British Museum, all our papyri would have been lost.

A second fire, the cause of which remained undetermined, broke out three months later, on the 25th May 1956, in a room formerly occupied by Egyptology in Foster Court. It was now in the hands of contractors for restoration following the earlier conflagration. Sixteen rooms used by four departments had to be evacuated, and it was not until 1957 that the building could be reoccupied.

Not surprisingly, precautions were now drawn up in consultation with the London Fire Brigade. Experience with the two catastrophes led to the conclusion that the instruction: 'If you see a fire try to put it out', should contain the additional sentence: 'But if before entering a room you think that the room is on fire, do not open the door but dial the Lodge ...'. A second conclusion was that nightwatchmen and cleaners must be issued with master keys, for they had not been able to enter the laboratory as Egyptology had put on its own lock. It was categorically stated: 'Departments should not be allowed to put on their own locks. If departments wish to keep cleaners out for some particular reason they can inform the Establishment Officer accordingly'.

Meanwhile, the Provost had successfully negotiated with Professor Robertson of Archaeology for the removal of his casts of Classical statues, so that the Petrie Collection could expand into the second stable. Sir Ifor had put forward a series of powerful arguments, with the conclusion: 'I have also been thinking that Arkell is the only person who can catalogue the material, and that the period he will be with us is limited and diminishing'.

23. *The Edwards Library and the Pottery Room, c. 1960. On the right, Mr. Eric Uphill, then a postgraduate student of the Department. (Property of the Petrie Museum, UCL.)*

It was in October 1957 that Egyptology relinquished its post-fire quarters in Foster Court and completed its move to the opposite side. The Edwards Library was newly arranged and the outer museum gallery, always dubbed 'the Pottery Room', could be filled with ceramics once the sturdy and internally lighted new cases, paid for by the Hill bequest, arrived (Figure 23). Eric Uphill remembers 'trayloads of Badarian and other pottery carried at high risk across the court'. He assisted both in this exercise and in the moving of heavy stelae, and can report that all arrived safely. Martin Burgess gained a new laboratory, situated on the first floor of 4, Malet Place, for 'the restoration of objects and storage for highly flammable liquids'. A year later, and again in 1961, a further sum of £5500 was made available for seventeen tall, internally lighted 'inscription cases' (see Figure 22). This meant that by the time Arkell retired there were a total of seventy-one exhibit cases.

What was museum work really like in the fifties? Mr. Burgess has given me a graphic description of what he calls 'the daily round'. He begins with the retrieval, by Arkell and himself, of a few crates from Foster Court. 'We both got filthy dirty, sooty and black,

struggling in that terrible dark basement with two miserable little bulbs getting those packing cases out, which were thick with London dirt. They had been put up on bricks to try and dry them out from the flooding of the toilets next door.' As the boxes were 'stacked absolutely from floor to ceiling', the two men could not see what was there. A torch was essential, and cobwebs had to be brushed aside to read the numbers which had been written by Miss Lafleur on the side of each tea-chest. To get just one out normally necessitated moving ten other heavy containers. For a big move, porters from the Works Department were employed.

Once in the museum a nail-pulling jemmy and a hammer were used to open them, and the objects were quickly loaded into the cupboards, arranged after the type of material. Both men became 'terribly good' at the identification game. They would find joins and matches, and although salt had frequently destroyed the original markings, much detective work was still possible. Arkell compiled a card index for this purpose, noting, for instance, that Quibell invariably marked his objects with a very thick black Indian inkpen. The Curator then left tiny labels in each box.

On the 6th October 1961 the last of the crates was unpacked. It had taken ten years of herculean labour. The Provost was delighted: 'We are deeply indebted to you for the skill which you have brought in dealing with this difficult task'. As time went on and Arkell saw his retirement looming, he began to catalogue faster and faster, devoting more and more of his time to the task. Seven thousand seven hundred objects had been accessioned when he took over; when he left he had added about the same amount. Burgess wrote the inventory numbers on the objects, for which he used artist's oil paint, the most durable material. It was hoped that his large numbers would ensure future legibility, and thus prevent the identification problems which they had encountered.

According to Burgess, Arkell's rule was that 'the antiquities came first, but their use was the most important thing about them'. Serious students, in whatever field, were always welcome, and received permission to publish any object, provided that due acknowledgement was made to UCL. In the year ending in November 1962 there were thirty-five foreign visitors - which should be compared with the four hundred and fifty-five of 1991.

During these years one major loan is known to have taken place. In 1962 Predynastic ivory horns, the Ebony Negress (see Figure 25), and one of the Hawara portraits were on show at the Arts Council exhibition, 'Five Thousand Years of Egyptian Art', held at the Royal Academy in London. A year earlier Arkell had transferred the human bones from Qau, which showed disease and mended fractures, to the Department of Palaeontology at the British Museum of Natural History. This gift became the nucleus of their large reference collection.

Back in 1956 for the first time a College Photographer had been appointed, and thus began the Department's close relations with the present Photography and Illustration Centre, lately under the supervision of Mr. Peter Harrison. Before this time outside photographers had to be brought in by visiting scholars, and often they had to come back when their results turned out to be unsatisfactory. As this was naturally time-consuming for Arkell and Burgess, the appointment of Mr. Eric Hitchcock proved a 'tremendous bonus' to Egyptology.

The museum technician's skills were many and varied. One of his main tasks was the soaking of all the salty pottery, which he dried in the cool oven he had built in his laboratory. Breakages were mended with celluloid, a particular nightmare being the many smashed stone bowls scattered over eight tea-chests. A major exercise was his work on the bead collection (a subject on which Arkell was a world authority). The beads had been coated with a celluloid solution before the War, and were so shiny and sticky that they stuck together. Burgess first soaked them in acetone and then restrung over seven hundred necklaces. He mounted these on slats in the new beadcases. By the time he left he had treated well over two thousand objects, but Arkell could only conclude that: 'The collection will probably always need the attention of a full-time skilled restorer'.

The vicissitudes of the Petrie Collection were by no means over. There was the pitched and skylighted glass roof over the Shoolbred's stables, which caused leaks from the beginning. In 1967, for instance, blocked drains lead to a major flood which irretrievably damaged some cartonnage masks. Once again, the British Museum gave prompt aid. Then in 1958 there was the installation of a new central boiler house beneath the Department, resulting in 'noise and vibration', as the College Committee minutes put it, 'the latter being obnoxious for the Egyptian antiquities'. To cope with the latter, the display cases and storage units were insulated with felt. This became infested with moth which got such a hold that in the end it all had to be removed. There were also complaints about the stench, aggravated by the fact that the windows were firmly barred, but an investigation failed to detect any fumes. Whatever, the museum was now consistently too warm and the atmosphere too dry for the stability of the objects.

Emery often used to tell the story of how, prior to the installation, he was approached by Hector Corfiato, the Professor of Architecture, who told him that supporting the floors of the Petrie Museum while the work was in progress threatened to be massively expensive. Corfiato offered to build for Emery a new Egyptology Department and Museum to his own design at whatever expense, if only he would remove the collection and allow demolition of the Shoolbred's stables. Emery, however, asked where the antiquities were to be stored and where the students were to be taught in the interim - there was at the time no conceivable answer. Later, he came to think that an opportunity had been lost. In 1962 and again two years later he pressed for an additional storey to be built on top of the existing building, so that the entire first floor could be devoted to a museum with the offices and library above. The idea was mooted once more in 1968. Although technical advice was commissioned, estimates obtained, and the plans approved, the necessary funds were never forthcoming.

A more enjoyable subject is the person of Dr. Margaret Murray, still an unforgettable figure to those who were at the College in the fifties. Many people remember to this day the picture of her tiny four foot ten frame alongside the towering six foot two figure of Professor Emery. The stories surrounding her are legendary; two will have to suffice here.

According to Professor Plumley, Emery visited her in University College Hospital after an emergency appendicitis operation performed when she was in her nineties. He found her ensconced in her own private room, already sitting up in bed and typing furiously. That morning, she informed him, the French police had visited her, seeking her advice on a case of witchcraft in their country. Indeed, she had become a celebrated, albeit highly controversial authority on the subject, her *The Witch-Cult in Western Europe* (1921) being described as 'revolutionary' and 'epoch-making'.

The second anecdote is told by Eric Uphill and concerns another visit to her by Emery, accompanied by his secretary, when she was in her late nineties. Just as they were leaving she remarked: 'You know I've got an incurable disease?' Thinking that something very serious had developed, they were understandably relieved when she continued: 'Yes, old age'.

Ifor Evans acted as her well-wisher and champion from the moment he became Provost, thinking out all manner of ingenious schemes for her comfort and recognition. In 1952 he wanted to apply for a Civil List Pension for her, but this idea was quashed by Margaret Murray herself; she considered her small pension adequate for her needs. Later plans for recommending her for a C.B.E. and obtaining the Petrie Medal (see page 21) for her were likewise thwarted. However, in 1960 Sir Ifor induced her to accept £100 from an obscure College fund, for grants to professors of distinction inadequately rewarded in their day, to increase her pension. The receipt of some unexpected royalties later made her anxious to repay this sum, and it took all Sir Ifor's powers of cajolery to persuade her to

use it to purchase a dictaphone for her work. Often, when he had not seen her in the College for some time, he would show his affection by writing simply to ascertain how she was keeping. Every year he used to send her roses on her birthday, harrying as many other people as possible into remembering the occasion.

Then, in 1961, the Margaret Murray Portrait Appeal was launched. A bronze cast of her head by the sculptor Stephen Rickard had been commissioned privately by her old pupil Dr. Violet MacDermot (see page 60). The first cast was made for submission at the Royal Academy's Summer Exhibition of that year, and the casting of the second copy, taken at the same time, was underwritten by UCL. The Appeal sought to raise the £150 needed, but the target was surpassed, the excess being used for a standing pedestal to support the bronze on its black marble base. Plans for a plaque (her name is etched only in hieroglyphs on the bronze itself) have only materialized in this Centenary year. There was no unveiling ceremony, perhaps because, as Dr. MacDermot told me, Margaret Murray was not her 'usual sparkling self' at the time, and the work fails to do her justice. She herself was not particularly impressed when she came to view it in the Pottery Room, in its original location facing out towards the Edwards Library.

This inspired Professor Emery to secure a cast of Percival Ball's alabaster bust of Amelia Edwards in the National Portrait Gallery (Frontispiece), so that the foundress would also be represented in the Department. In May 1961 the Friends of UCL gave £20 to cover the cost of a plaster cast, made by a craftsman in the British Museum. Originally placed in the Edwards Library, it now resides in the Pottery Room.

Margaret Murray's mind continued to remain as active as ever. Eric Uphill remembers that, until the age of ninety-four when the many stairs began to defeat her, she appeared regularly in the Department, occasionally invading one of Faulkner's language classes, and invariably wanting to see a particular object in the museum. When she was ninety-eight, she wrote to Emery: 'I am doing a bit of research on the Hierakonpolis finds with what are, to me, surprising results'. Two years later, only a few weeks before her death, she sent him another letter, asking many detailed questions for her 'Hierakonpolis work'. In 1961 she was forced to enter for the remainder of her life the Queen Victoria Memorial Hospital at Welwyn in Hertfordshire, where, although badly crippled by arthritis, she continued writing, and published two books in her hundredth year, one of which was her autobiography.

With her hundredth birthday approaching, Sir Ifor came up with imaginative suggestions of how it should be celebrated. Plans to make her a Dame, or to hire a coach for the Professorial Board to go and greet her, were soon abandoned, and it was arranged that the centenarian herself would be brought by her doctor to UCL on Monday 15th July 1963, two days after her birthday. An illuminator was commissioned to prepare the resolution passed by the Professorial Board a month earlier to record its thanks and appreciation. The text aptly describes her as Petrie's 'right hand', who, by relieving him of a great part of his teaching commitments, had made possible the vast output of his fieldwork. Sir Ifor circulated copies of the resolution to the London Press, and *The Times* was invited to send a photographer to the event, which would take the form of a buffet luncheon in the Provost's Room, organized by Margaret Drower.

Margaret Murray's own preparations had involved a consultation with the Queen's hat designer, who had visited her at the Hospital with a selection from his range. She arrived for her party wearing a very fetching toque. Surrounded by thirty of her friends and pupils - among those present were Emery and Faulkner (Figure 24), Mrs. Engelbach, Harding, Miss Lafleur, Lady Thornton, Miss Tufnell, Uphill, and Sir Mortimer Wheeler - she managed, despite her deafness and the confines of a wheelchair, to talk to many people, fully remembering everyone. At the appropriate moment the College Chef ceremoniously carried in the cake which had been designed by Miss Drower. Decorated in marzipan were her initials 'M. A. M.', together with the appropriate hieroglyphs for 'life, prosperity, and health', and the year 'one hundred'. Later Dr. Murray received her citation (Figure 24). Elegantly inscribed on vellum, in black, red, blue, and burnished gold, it now resides in the College Library. After a short speech

24. *Margaret Murray at her hundredth birthday celebration luncheon at UCL; above: joking with Professor Emery (centre) and Dr. Faulkner (right); below: reading her citation, July 1963. (Courtesy of The Times Newspapers Ltd.)*

of acknowledgement, she departed from UCL for the last time. Exactly four months later to the day after her birthday, she died.

In September 1963 the sixty-five year old Reverend Dr. Arkell retired from the College to embark on a fourth career as a Church of England clergyman. He had been ordained in 1960, having always wanted to enter the ministry at the end of his life and so to follow in his father's footsteps. Five years earlier he had been awarded a Doctor of Literature Degree by the University of Oxford.

Arkell held his Buckinghamshire living until his final retirement in 1971, being as popular as in all the other fields he had pursued. He remained an Honorary Research Associate of the Department, and it was my privilege to show this remarkable man my own work in the museum on an occasion shortly before his death in 1980.

Martin Burgess also left in 1963, but he stayed on until Christmas in order to see the new Honorary Curator fully ensconced. He had married Arkell's daughter Eleanor that October, a timing which prevented him from having to work for his father-in-law. He is now a well-known clock-maker, his inspiration partly deriving from his handling of so many Egyptian antiquities. His successor Stephen Harris was a young conservator still under training at the Institute of Archaeology, where he carried out most of his work. He left after two years to take up a position in Bristol.

Arkell had been anxious for a proper and leisurely handover of the collection to his successor in order to prevent a return to the confusions which he had inherited. He had pressed Emery for this from 1960 onwards, presuming that the new appointee would be of junior lecturer status, with time to bring his work to fruition. But Emery and the Provost had other plans. Their aim was to replace Arkell's personal readership by an established position, and to obtain someone who would strenuously develop the Department's teaching. The new member of staff would also be in charge of the Petrie Collection and serve as acting Head of Department when the professor was excavating. Once the post was established, the name of H. S. Smith was put forward to the University without competition and he was duly appointed.

Henry (Harry) Smith, like Edwards and Plumley before him, had been a pupil at Merchant Taylors' School. His father Sidney Smith (see page 14) had been one of Margaret Murray's students, and he himself was a pupil of Glanville. His mentor had once referred to him as being 'in the all-rounder tradition of the giants of the past', as his thorough competence in both the archaeological and philological fields had now become a rare phenomenon. Smith was at that moment Lecturer in Egyptology in the Faculty of Oriental Studies, Cambridge, and Lady Wallis Budge Fellow and Acting Tutor to undergraduates at Christ's College. He already had nine years teaching experience. As he had worked for ten years with Emery in both Egypt and Nubia, it was felt that he could assist the Edwards Professor in the field and play a major part in the publication of his past, present, and future reports. In December 1962 Sir Ifor was able to approach Smith himself telling him: 'You may know that Professor Emery himself has long wished to see you in this new Readership and feels that the development of our very flourishing Department of Egyptology would depend largely on your presence in London'. Indeed, from Smith's arrival in October 1963 on the Department began to grow in a way it had never previously envisaged.

One of the first problems faced by the new reader was that of the Gardiner bequest, which on its arrival in 1964 was stated to be the most important gift of books made to UCL in the course of the century. It was certainly the most outstanding Egyptological library to have remained in private hands, being especially rich in many valuable and unobtainable works of the last century. During his lifetime Sir Alan Gardiner, short of space for the ever increasing number of publications he acquired, had promised about five hundred volumes to the Griffith Institute in Oxford, some of which had already been handed over. He now wanted to do the same for UCL, for as he said: 'I have a deep interest in the Edwards' Library since it was there where I commenced my studies about 1895' (see page 13). But, as Faulkner had asked for textbooks, and these were the very ones that Gardiner needed to retain for himself, the matter became a stalemate.

Then in 1962 the College Librarian, Mr. Joseph Scott, visited Gardiner at his home at Iffley, Oxford. It was arranged that the latter should make a new will (for his will of 1934, see page 29-30), under which his library should go to UCL, while surplus books not needed for the Edwards Library should be offered first to Cambridge, secondly to Liverpool, and, finally, to any other 'worthwhile collections of

Egyptology books' in Great Britain.

On the 16th December 1963 Smith wrote to Scott expressing his concern that no priority had been attached to the scheme for the extension of the Department, for if the Gardiner Library arrived there would be no accommodation available. Three days later he had to despatch a second hasty missive informing the Librarian that Gardiner had just died and the matter was now urgent. Early in 1964, Scott wrote to Gardiner's son: 'I should like to let you know at the outset that we at this end are in no particular hurry'. The reality was that it was not yet known how to cope with the four thousand volumes of the bequest! Fortunately, Scott soon discovered ten large bookcases, surplus to the requirements of Exeter University, which were being sold at cost price, and he managed to acquire the funds to purchase these.

In order to be scrupulously fair to the remaining institutions, the Department only chose books it did not already possess. Thus some one thousand eight hundred volumes entered the Edwards Library, each now distinguished by a bookplate for which as Gardiner's title: 'President of the Egypt Exploration Society' was chosen. But it was not until 1972 that the distribution to other Egyptological libraries was finally resolved. Cambridge and Liverpool having chosen their share, Durham was then approached, with Swansea taking the remainder. Certain travel and ornithology books went to Gardiner's grandchildren.

There were two further bequests to the Edwards Library during the sixties. In 1968 Miss Jane Somers Cocks left her books, lecture notes, photographic material, and even a few genuine Egyptian antiquities to the University with instructions that they were to be retained together. She had graduated from UCL in 1929 with a degree in Archaeology, specializing in Egyptology. As Faulkner had then given her extra tuition in Egyptian and Coptic, it was appropriate that Smith should have recommended the acceptance of her bequest by the Department. The eighty or so volumes are basic textbooks, of considerable value to the students.

A year later the Warden of College Hall deposited over a hundred books and periodicals on permanent loan. These came mainly from the Mary Brodrick bequest (see page 19). Mention should also be made of a Margaretta Kirby Fund, created from the £7000 residuary estate of this ex-student (see page 38) who had died in 1962. As stated in her will, the income of this trust fund is used 'for the furtherance of Studies or Research Work in Egyptology'. Miss Kirby's books also entered the library, one being the valuable folio volume of Budge's *The Book of the Dead. Facsimile of the Papyrus of Ani in the British Museum* (1894).

The new reader had been instructed to extend and develop the Department's teaching, and to review its courses in order to bring them into line with modern standards. This was particularly necessary with regard to the old Academic Diploma in Egyptology which, as it gave no degree, fitted ill with the changing pattern of qualifications and of government grants. For the moment, however, Emery wanted this still to be retained.

The bulk of the teaching now fell to Smith who was soon giving twelve hours of classes a week, in addition to undertaking all the research supervision, and acting as Departmental Tutor. He taught the 'Religion' and 'Small antiquities' (soon renamed 'Material Cultures and Typology) courses, and before long added 'History', together with some language for Faulkner. He also spent two months every Spring Term as Emery's assistant at Saqqara.

The student body now increased to an annual average of ten or more and the general quality certainly improved. The following British students in the Emery era subsequently held important Egyptological posts: Miss Carol Andrews, Assistant Keeper in the Department of Egyptian Antiquities at the British Museum; Miss Janine Bourriau (now Mrs. French), formerly Keeper of Antiquities at the Fitzwilliam Museum, Cambridge; Dr. Rosalie David, Keeper of Egyptology at the Manchester Museum, University of Manchester; Professor Geoffrey Martin, sixth Edwards Professor; and Mr. Anthony Mills, Director of the Dakhla Oasis Project. Some of the foreign alumni of this era were: Dr. Faiza Haikal, Vice-President of the International Association of Egyptologists (IAE); Professor Cathleen Keller, Professor of Egyptology at the University of California at Berkeley; Dr. Robert Merrillees, Australian Diplomat and Cypriot pottery expert; and Professor David O'Connor, Professor of Egyptology at the University of Pennsylvania, Philadelphia. Mention should also be made of Dr. Ali el-Khouli, a senior official in the Egyptian Antiquities Organization

(E. A. O.), who, although he did not study for his doctorate until the next régime, was Emery's loyal assistant in the field.

Smith's brief was to complete the identification, cataloguing, exhibition, and conservation of the collection. On his arrival the Petrie Museum had achieved some semblance of the appearance which it has today, but there was a great deal still to be done and major decisions to be made. Both the display and storage were still only provisional; an integrated, overall plan was now required. Smith soon realized that the heavy stelae and sculptures, together with all the pottery, must be retained as Arkell had left them (see Figures 22 and 23), there being no other suitably large cabinets. On the other hand, the various 'pyramid' cases (see Figure 21) were only suitable for small objects. A final dictate was the general lack of space which meant that the normal type of 'art-historical' or 'culture-historical' approach was here not possible. A firm decision was taken to stick to Petrie's principles of showing as much as possible, and to exhibit and store material together which came from one site or belonged to one of Petrie's catalogue categories. This meant that it was possible to allow either a chronological overview of domestic and funerary artefact assemblages, together with a comprehensive idea of the material from each site, or to illustrate the technical and decorative developments shown in Petrie's object groups. A new typed card catalogue, with cross-indexing, was now introduced in addition to the handwritten registers. This has been the mainstay of the museum's documentation ever since.

However, a major disruption was caused in this orderly progress, which was to set the whole process back several years. This was the arrival of the Wellcome Collection in 1964. Assembled by the late Sir Henry Wellcome, it belonged to the Wellcome Historical Medical Museum, although much of the Egyptian section had little if anything to do with medicine. In 1960 David Dixon had been appointed to classify the objects. Originally the museum intended to sell the material in the United States, but Dixon brought advance news of this to his old teacher Professor Emery, who, feeling that it would be wrong if it left Britain, prevailed upon the Trustees to present the entire Egyptian assemblage to UCL.

The Wellcome Collection arrived still housed in its three hundred and fifty packing cases, having been in off-site storage since 1946. It was accompanied by ten large 'pyramid' and one table case, and two cupboards, all still in use. Dixon was given full facilities to continue his work, becoming an Honorary Research Associate of the Department. Space had to be found in the museum's already crowded cupboards for the new antiquities. This necessitated packing the Petrie Collection much more tightly into fewer drawers and cupboards, thus destroying Arkell's provisional arrangements. It was at this point that a second storey for the Department was again mooted. Work on the Wellcome Collection eventually came to a complete standstill and the bulk remained stored in the basements of Foster Court and in a Tottenham Court Road annexe.

The situation became so acute and the proper utilization of the Petrie Collection so impeded, that in 1970 Smith agreed a dispersal scheme with the Wellcome Trustees. Other Egyptological institutions in Britain would be given the material, only that directly relating to the Department's own interests being retained. Thus antiquities from sites dug by Petrie and his School were kept, but these constituted merely a small proportion of the whole. The principal beneficiaries were the Liverpool City Museum and the University of Swansea Museum. The Birmingham City Museum and the Gulbenkian Museum of the University of Durham also gained some objects.

Another time-consuming operation in these years was the distribution of material from Nubia and Saqqara, representing the E. E. S.'s share of antiquities from the divisions of the Sudanese and Egyptian Governments. Although handled mainly by the British Museum, part of the activity also took place at UCL. Thus, during the sixties, the Petrie Museum was to gain its fine collections from Buhen and Qasr Ibrim and, as a direct result of Emery's negotiations and 'admirable relations' with the Egyptian authorities, a splendid range of Late Period sculpture, bronzes, ritual and dedicatory objects from the Second Animal Necropolis at North Saqqara.

In 1965 artefacts from some of Petrie's digs in Palestine were transferred to the Western Asiatic Department at the British Museum to grace the new Palestinian Room. In the same year the College Committee accepted the 'Langton Egyptian Collection' offered by Mrs. Blanche Langton, who hoped it would 'encourage further study into the cult of the cat'. Formed by Mrs. Langton and her late husband, she handed it over two years before her own death in 1972. In accordance with the terms of the bequest, it is exhibited in a specially constructed display area in the main room of the museum.

In 1968 a committee of the Museums and Galleries Commission, after a visit to the various College collections, proposed as the only possibility, that a new floor should be built above the Department. Its conclusion was: 'Until a permanent new building is available there can be no thought of this museum's adapting itself to the use of a wider public'. How well we have managed to achieve this despite remaining in our stables, will become apparent in the next chapter.

Staff changes in the mid-sixties began with the replacement of Stephen Harris by a new Museum Assistant in October 1965. Miss Barbara Bishop (now Mrs. Adams, the Curator of the Petrie Museum) was then a young assistant at the British Museum of Natural History. It was to be a most crucial appointment, for with her arrival the real transformation of the Petrie Collection from a Departmental teaching and research tool into a true university museum began.

A few months earlier Miss Joyce Townend had become Research Assistant. Having first entered the College as a student in 1925, she had thereafter acted as Research Assistant to David M. S. Watson, the Professor of Zoology, who had continued his work at UCL for fourteen years after retiring from his chair. His final departure had left the sixty-two year old Miss Townend without a rôle in that department, and Egyptology was fortunate to secure her part-time appointment. During the next nine years, this trained cataloguer and skilled draughtswoman was to undertake the detailed sorting, identification, and registration of much site material in the museum. According to Julia Samson, 'her work in Egyptology was of such depth, that one would not have known that she had not been in it all her life'. Ill-health forced her to resign from her 'immensely enjoyable' job in 1974, just one year before she would have completed fifty years service. She died two months later.

In 1966 Julia Samson (see page 38-9) had returned to the museum after an absence of twenty-seven years. A year later she was appointed Honorary Research Assistant working three days a week, her special task being to write a catalogue of the Amarna collection.

As regards the teaching staff, Faulkner retired in 1967, at the age of seventy-three. In 1960 he had been awarded a Doctor of Literature Degree by the University of London; a year later he became a Fellow of UCL, having been nominated by his old teacher, Dr. Margaret Murray, who once, referring to his language skills, had said to him: 'Young man, you know too much'. After his retirement, he undertook his most prolific work and produced the first standard English translations of all three major compendia of funerary spells: the Pyramid Texts, the Coffin Texts, and the Book of the Dead. On his death in 1983 he left his books for the eventual benefit of his old Department, to which he had remained connected as an Honorary Research Associate. This Faulkner Library has retained its separate identity and has been used for the benefit of staff and students ever since. His place was immediately filled by Dr. David Dixon, then at the end of his Wellcome Fellowship, who became a full lecturer and took over from Smith as the Honorary Curator of the Petrie Museum.

Finally, a few words should be devoted to Emery's loyal secretary Miss K. E. Cynthia Cox who had been appointed in 1953 following the resignation of Mrs. Carroll. She had previously acted as secretary to both the Headmaster of Wellingborough School and the Headmistress of Roedean. For five years she had worked for the Heads of the Arts Departments at Birkbeck College. At the same time, she attended evening classes there. So she gained a degree in Modern History from the University of London in 1952 when she was fifty years of age. She promptly registered for a Master of Arts Degree which she obtained within four years. Miss Cox arrived at UCL with glowing references from her former employers, one of whom described her as 'a treasure'. The Headmistress of Roedean was particularly impressed by the fact that: 'this well-educated, well-read woman ... has the social gifts needed for receiving and interviewing callers of all kinds ... [moreover], she plays an excellent game of tennis'.

Miss Cox had an amusingly detached and somewhat cynical view of the value of Egyptology or indeed of ancient studies. Her heart was in the eighteenth and early nineteenth centuries A. D., and not B. C. As a historical novelist of some repute, she published *The Enigma of the Age* (1966), a lucid account of the extraordinary life of the Chevalier d'Eon, an agent of the inner secret service of Louis XV.

By 1964 she had become a tragic victim of Parkinson's disease. Despite gallant efforts to continue her work, she was forced to retire in 1967. Seven years later she died. She was succeeded by Miss Anthea Page who was half-way through the Extra-Mural Department's Diploma in Archaeology.

Emery retired in 1970, having twice had his appointment extended. He was now sixty-seven. Three years earlier he had undergone a serious surgical operation, but, in typical fashion, he was off to his beloved Saqqara after only six weeks convalescence. It had meant, however, that his teaching was even more restricted than before. In 1969 he had been awarded the C.B.E. (Commander of the Order of the British Empire), and on his retirement the title of Emeritus Professor of Egyptology was conferred on him. Due to his intensive archaeological activity he now had an enormous backlog of unpublished excavation reports. Before his retirement Lord Evans had privately assured Emery that the College would give him a research post in the Department so he could complete this essential work. He was therefore appointed Margaretta Kirby Senior Research Fellow from the 1st October 1970.

Only six months later, on the 7th March 1971, although he had seemed fitter than at any time since his operation, he collapsed suddenly in the midst of his Saqqara campaign. A second stroke two days later was followed by his death on the 11th March. This was the way in which he would have wished to meet his end, pursuing that romantic passion for discovery nourished since boyhood. The fourth Edwards Professor is buried in the land in which he had served as a soldier and a diplomat, and from which as an archaeologist he had unearthed so many treasures.

Emery's twenty years of unremittingly successful fieldwork had gained the Department and the College great renown, for, like his illustrious predecessor, his work had covered the whole of Egyptian history and it had changed the face of that history. There can be no greater tribute than that, by 1970, the Department's public and academic reputation had resumed the status which it had enjoyed in Petrie's great days.

Chapter Nine

Epilogue
1970~1992

In January 1970, with Professor Emery's retirement imminent, the name of Henry S. Smith, the Reader in the Department, was put forward without competition to the University. Thus he became the fifth Edwards Professor that October. As the appointment had been an internal one, it had been possible to advertise a lectureship to bring the teaching staff back up to three. Dr. Geoffrey T. Martin was the successful candidate. A UCL graduate in Ancient History, he had gained his doctorate at Cambridge, and was at that juncture Lady Wallis Budge Fellow at Christ's College. He possessed excellent field experience, having assisted Emery in the Sudan and in Egypt every year since 1963. Smith now took leave of absence to direct the Egypt Exploration Society's excavations at Saqqara for the first academic term and Martin for the second, a pattern that was to continue for the next eighteen years.

These heavy field commitments dissuaded Smith from introducing a full undergraduate degree in Egyptology. However, he immediately instituted a two-year postgraduate Master of Philosophy Degree, so that, with Emery's departure, the Academic Diploma in Egyptology, which was now attracting very few students indeed, could at last be phased out (see page 82). However, after a decade, the new qualification was likewise discontinued. As with its predecessor, it had become increasingly difficult to obtain a grant for what was essentially an introductory course.

In 1980 a combined Bachelor of Arts Degree in Ancient History and Egyptology was introduced to replace the old arrangement with the History Department; this has proved most successful. Four years later, the Hebrew with Egyptian Degree was redesigned and renamed 'Ancient Egyptian and Biblical Hebrew'. Then in 1990, under the sixth Edwards Professor, the rigid syllabuses of these undergraduate degrees were revised and transformed into the Course-Unit system giving students a much wider choice of options in their combination of Ancient World papers. The result has been a surge in the popularity of these courses.

The appointment of two additional lecturers, a linguist and an archaeologist (see page 93), meant that the teaching could be greatly expanded. Therefore, 1991 saw the introduction of a Master of Arts Degree in Coptic and Demotic studies, the first of its kind in Britain, and a Bachelor of Arts Degree in Egyptian Archaeology. The latter includes general archaeological topics taught at the Institute of Archaeology, and a wide range of Egyptology options. It is hoped that this degree will fulfil the long-felt need for excavators trained in modern scientific archaeology, yet with sufficient specialized knowledge to work successfully in the Nile Valley. Petrie would rejoice to know that the wheel has turned once again full circle to the days of the 1910 Training Course (see page 11-12), and that his unrivalled collection is still being used to teach countless UCL students the culture of Ancient Egypt by direct contact with its artefacts.

The intrepid prehistorian and Petrie 'Pup' Dr. Gertrude Caton-Thompson (see page 22-3) died in 1985 at the age of ninety-seven, having become a Fellow of the College just a year earlier. She left her residuary estate to UCL for the general scientific work of her old Department, subject to the prior interest of a life tenant who died two years later. Valued at over £100,000 at the date of transfer, the income from this, the most munificent bequest ever to have been received, is used to provide fellowships and grants, both of which bear her name. The Caton-Thompson Fund has already made a great and salutory difference to the chances for students and academic staff to pursue various projects, and has also been used for urgent museum conservation work.

Back in 1982 a smaller sum had been received from the estate of Mr. Reginald Clover, an evening class student of the author, who subsequently became one of the museum's voluntary workers. It was used to purchase four new textile storage units, together with a book display cabinet which is now sited in the foyer of the Department. Two commemorative plaques acknowledge the bequest.

The seventies renewed the long tradition initiated by Petrie of the publication of the archaeological wealth of his collection (see page 19-20). Miss Anthea Page, the Departmental Secretary, had suggested a young couple, Adrian and Lucinda Phillips, who were just setting up in business, as possible publishers for Julia Samson's book on the Amarna material. This duly appeared in 1972, the first in a series of new catalogues to be published by Messrs. Aris and Phillips. Written by members of the Department, they comprise those on Hierakonpolis and Gurob by Barbara Adams and Angela Thomas respectively; Anthea Page's own two books on the sculpture and figured ostraca; and the three-volumed publication of the stelae, together with that on the mummy cases and funerary cones, by Harry Stewart. Other minor works are those by Adams on the Koptos sculptured pottery, and by Martin and Raisman on the canopic equipment. It is difficult to see how these not readily saleable catalogues, together with other volumes in the 'Modern Egyptology' series, would otherwise have achieved publication. The same firm also published Smith's Inaugural Lecture, delivered on the 6th March 1973. Entitled 'Memphis Under the Last of the Pharaohs', it appears in his *A Visit to Ancient Egypt* (1974, page 1-20).

As official publishers to the Department, Aris and Phillips also produced much-needed reprints of eight of Petrie's more important object catalogues and site publications, originally issued under the auspices of the British School of Archaeology in Egypt. Substantial annual royalties from these reprints were paid into the Petrie Fund, supplementing those sums already received since 1953 from Bernard Quaritch Ltd., the original publishers to the B.S.A.E. (see page 74).

Thus it became possible to provide, apart from the Flinders Petrie Scholarship, special grants to students in particular need. Despite this, such a considerable income had accumulated in this account that recently the possibility arose of creating new awards known as the Flinders Petrie Grants in Egyptian Archaeology. Presented throughout the year to enable the Department's undergraduates to visit Egypt, the first four recipients undertook their study tour during the Christmas vacation in 1991.

The fabric of the Shoolbred's stables continued to worsen over the years. A combination of excess heating and dryness, coupled with the constantly leaking roof above, and vibrations and smut from the boiler house below, as well as general London grime, meant that the collection was steadily deteriorating. There were several major summer floods during the seventies and early eighties, causing thousands of pounds worth of damage. A committee of the Museums and Galleries Commission once again visited the collection in 1975, and subsequently issued another adverse report on the building and its environment (see page 84).

The College recognized that these conditions were desperate. The Todd-Cox Plan of 1972 would, under its second stage, have demolished the stables and rehoused Egyptology in purpose-built accommodation; alas, this phase was postponed indefinitely due to lack of finances. However, in 1979 the sixth Provost, Sir James Lighthill, decreed that Egyptology would be one of the four major elements in the College's 150th Anniversary Appeal. This aimed to complete the restoration of certain areas of UCL still suffering from the ravages of the London Blitz. The ambitious idea was to refurbish the top (third) floor of Foster Court for the Department. Architect's plans were drawn up for a much enlarged, purpose-built, environmentally controlled modern museum, to be divided into display and working areas, and even including its own archive room. Alongside were an expanded Edwards Library, spacious offices, and greatly improved teaching space. The escalating cost of this was soon estimated at £700,000, for which no money was available from government or university sources.

It was not until October 1981 that the Appeal, delayed in the hopes of better times to come, was finally launched, in the presence of Princess Anne on the day she was installed

25. *The Queen Mother, during her visit to UCL, discusses with Professor Smith (right) the Ebony Negress, June 1983. (Courtesy of the Photography & Illustration Centre, UCL.)*

as Chancellor of the University of London. On this occasion, Her Royal Highness was treated to a special display of some of our treasures. In June 1983 it was the turn of the Queen Mother, the previous Chancellor, to visit UCL, in order to attend an informal luncheon marking the commencement of work on new buildings at the Gower Street frontage, one of the aims of the Appeal. In addition to viewing these plans, she was shown prized items from the Petrie Museum (Figure 25). After lunch Her Majesty met a number of staff and students at coffee in the Margaret Murray Room and was presented with a copy of Dr. Murray's *My First Hundred Years*. The involvement of Egyptology on this royal occasion was in many ways reminiscent of the visit of Queen Mary in 1927 (see page 21).

The project failed to attract major earmarked donations, only £8000 having been raised for Egyptology when the 150th Anniversary Appeal closed in 1984. A year later the Department was to take over its own fund-raising.

In the interim the College took the realistic decision to renovate the existing premises to the standard required by the Museums and Galleries Commission. Two schemes were put forward by the Bursar's Department, of which the more expensive was the one adopted. This allowed for the introduction of a suspended ceiling to cut out the effects of the glass roof and to hide the plant machinery of the environmental system, designed to maintain the temperature and relative humidity. At the same time measures were to be taken to steady the vibrating boilers below and to reduce the infiltration of smut. Ultra-violet screened lighting was to be installed, its controllable nature allowing a temporary heightening for visitors if required.

The College was to fund well over half the amount of this project, but it was up to the Department to find the remainder. Rapidly escalating building costs also meant that a strict time-limit had to be imposed on the fund-raising, which was masterminded by Professor Smith, assisted by his loyal secretary. The chief donor was the Museums and Galleries Commission which authorized its maximum capital grant of £25,000. Various charitable trusts and scientific institutions, commercial companies and many private individuals contributed. (The names of all the larger benefactors have been recorded on a plaque placed at the entrance to the newly-refurbished museum.) However, for eighteen months or so the issue hung in the balance and a 'final appeal' letter was circulated. Just at the moment when it seemed we must fail, albeit by a narrow margin, a key donation of £10,000 was received from Mr. Neil Kreitman, an American philanthropist. This ensured that the work could be put in hand in the summer vacation of 1986. By the time the museum opened two years later the Department had managed to raise the creditable sum of £71,000 (including the amount from the 150th Appeal).

Two projects were actually involved in the refurbishment, for the opportunity was being taken to enlarge and improve the Edwards Library, the cost of which was entirely borne by the College. In this connection it must here be mentioned that, back in 1975, an access door and corridor had been created from the first floor of the adjacent D. M. S. Watson

Library into the Edwards Library, thereby linking the two buildings for the first time. The aim was to improve security; the book losses from Egyptology, with its two doors opening directly onto Malet Place, had been considerable over the years. Although unsightly, the new entrance had the desired effect (despite an irreconcilable conflict with fire regulations), and allowed for much longer opening hours. At the same time the museum, having lost its dray-horse entrance, was able to concentrate more on its own internal security.

Now, in the summer of 1986, the books from the Edwards Library were moved to the ground and basement floors of the D. M. S. Watson building, where they mostly remained accessible to readers. The library was then enlarged, at the cost of the museum, the professor's room, and Faulkner's 'Rabbit-Hutch' (see page 74). The latter became considerably more cage-like, even before the present computer moved in. An improved entry system with a proper foyer was also created. The reshelved volumes were back in their place again for the start of the autumn term.

By this date the Pottery Room had also undergone refurbishment. It had originally been hoped to store the majority of the exhibited antiquities elsewhere, either in the College or in other museums, but this proved impossible. As the objects were to remain *in situ*, a two-phase operation became inevitable; three months before this commenced a major dismantling campaign had begun, undertaken by the museum staff, assisted by a stalwart band of volunteers. Initially, each pot was individually wrapped in acid-free tissue paper and bubble-wrap plastic before being crated with its fellows; an intricate recording system was maintained throughout. Then the main room had to be stripped and the numerous small and delicate objects stored in existing cupboard space, or wrapped and placed in further packing-cases. The momentum never slackened and the work was completed a week before the contractors were due to start. The pottery crates (two hundred and thirty in total) were placed in the main gallery while the first phase was underway, after which all the containers were transferred over to the Pottery Room, together with the moveable 'pyramid' cases (fortunately, the 'inscription' cases and their heavy contents could be boarded up and remain *in situ*). The entire refurbishment lasted six months.

Over a year was needed to remount the exhibition. This afforded an ideal opportunity to clarify the arrangement, the sequence of vitrines in the main room now running chronologically for the first time. Surplus material, particularly in the pottery cabinets and the Amarna section, could be ruthlessly 'pruned'; and, at the same time, some unfamiliar objects, such as the Wellcome Meroitic antiquities, were extracted from storage to broaden the display. Every individual object card was retyped, detailed typeset labels also being provided for each case. The white storage cupboards at the entrance to the now-reduced Pottery Room were removed to the rear, their place being taken by some rather more spectacular newly-conserved dresses and coffins. The effect is best summed up by the comment in a professional review: 'the immediate impression on entering the first room is now of a museum'.

Thus, after a two-year closure and a £180,000 renovation, the museum was ready for business once again. On the 24th May 1988 it was formally re-opened by Professor Sir Randolph Quirk, the previous Vice-Chancellor of the University, in the presence of the guest of honour, His Excellency the Ambassador of the Arab Republic of Egypt, Mr. Youssef Sharara. One of the hundred guests at the reception, held in the Housman Room, was Miss Lisette Petrie, the granddaughter of Sir Flinders Petrie, in the absence of her aunt, Miss Ann Petrie through ill-health. Among those present were some whose connections with the Department stretched back over many decades (Figure 26). In two groups the visitors walked over to the museum to view the new displays, which were favourably received. The evening will go down in the annals of the Department, and as such must be left to a future historian to evaluate. It is here best summed up in the words of the Provost, Sir James Lighthill, whose vision had enabled the event to come about, as: 'the auspicious reception for those who have helped the College with its marvellous Petrie Museum'.

Foremost among these were the indefatigable helpers without whom the arduous task of packing and remounting could never have been achieved. Many of them were long-standing volunteers, for the system had first been instituted in 1978. Teenagers and octogenarians have worked contented alongside

26. *Miss Margaret Drower (centre), Petrie's biographer, chats with Mrs. Julia Samson (right) at the re-opening of the refurbished Petrie Museum, May 1988. (Courtesy of the UCL Records Office.)*

one another, all contributing to the most basic tasks, and thereby relieving the curators of much administrative burden. Over the years these loyal assistants have proved their weight in gold, but at no time more so than during the refurbishment.

At the opening ceremony one of them was especially singled out. In recognition of his unstinting labour the Provost conferred on Mr. Harry Stewart the title of 'Sir Flinders Petrie Honorary Life Research Fellow'. A former student (see page 61), he had held concurrently a lectureship in archaeological drawing and surveying at the Institute of Archaeology, which led to his early involvement in teaching within the Department. In 1970 he was appointed an Honorary Research Fellow and began to work on his catalogues (see page 87). In the decade since his retirement, Mr. Stewart has been able to devote even more of his time to the museum. He is currently registering our shabti collection.

A last part of the renovations was still to be executed: a complete re-roofing. This was undertaken in two phases during 1989-90 in order finally to solve the problem of the recurrent flooding. During the work the displays had to be protected and covered, but, despite restricted viewing over two summers,

the museum remained open to the public.

It had soon become apparent that the improvements of 1986 were only to be achieved at a substantial cost. In leaving the antiquities *in situ* a calculated temporary risk had been accepted in exchange for the satisfactory long-term protection of the whole collection; also, moving the antiquities elsewhere would similarly have been fraught with dangers. After the ultra-dry atmosphere they had been used to, a damp winter spent in the museum with the heating turned off and no humidity control possible, caused inevitable damage. Previously stable artefacts did not escape, nor did those that had been treated earlier. In a process that held the remounting back by three months, every one of the eighty thousand objects in the collection had to be examined: over seventeen hundred had succumbed, including nearly four hundred pots which could be desalted in-house. (Breakages were, by contrast, absolutely minimal.) The large professional bill was found not to be covered by insurance, and the restoration had to be borne by the Department's nominal conservation grant. Since the rescue work had to take priority, the normal programme has been put back nearly ten years.

It is the state of the antiquities that has been our major concern over the last decades. The receipt of a triennial grant from the College enabled an arrangement to be set up with the Conservation Department at the Institute of Archaeology whereby in 1975 students started to work on our objects. This still continues, albeit on a reduced scale and only for special projects. Since 1980 the bulk of the treatment has been undertaken by Richard and Helena Jaeschke on a freelance basis. With their special understanding of the needs of Egyptian objects, our associated conservators have successfully restored much of Petrie's fragile heritage. Specialized work on textiles has been carried out in the Textile Conservation Centre at Hampton Court Palace, with which an on-going arrangement was set up a decade ago.

At its most spectacular, the work in recent years has resulted in the retrieval of objects which had been virtually lost to Egyptology. Three examples should suffice. A muddy, odorous bundle of linen rags undergoing treatment at the Victoria and Albert Museum, yielded the Tarkhan dress. The earliest garment in the world, it was once worn by a young Egyptian teenager around 2800 BC. Of a similar date are the Koptos lions, discovered by Barbara Adams as thousands of fragmentary limestone pieces. Originally excavated by Petrie in 1893-94 (see page 7-8), they were now lying in tea-chests in a store belonging to the Wellcome Historical Medical Museum. The Trustees subsequently presented the lions, together with four hundred accompanying objects from the same site, to UCL; thereby complementing the material given in 1964 (see page 83). Painstakingly conserved by Richard Jaeschke, the monumental pair, each weighing over half-a-ton, now stand guard outside the Provost's office.

Our forty Hawara mummy portraits are currently being cleaned, the final stage in a seventeen year project. In some cases the results have been surprising: the 'brown-robed' woman, perhaps our most beautiful painting, turned out to be dressed in blue. Even the most begrimed panel may, in the skilled hands of the Jaeschkes, reveal in a spectacular way the face of an inhabitant of the Fayum in Roman times.

In the mid-sixties the Petrie manuscripts, comprising his one hundred and fifty field notebooks, as well as tomb cards, journals, and distribution lists, had been gradually organized into an archive. In the early eighties the notebooks and tomb cards were transferred to microfiche to safeguard the fragile originals, written in (now fading) pencil, from wear and light. This was made possible by a £6000 grant from the Gulbenkian Foundation and the services of Mr. Robert Morkot, a graduate of UCL in Ancient History, who did the actual work. Institutions and individual scholars can now acquire copies of either full sets or of individual fiches. A few years later, the archive was augmented by Miss Ann Petrie when she presented to the museum her father's pocket diaries, together with a wealth of family correspondence, photographs, and other documents, among which was his Inaugural Lecture (Appendix 2).

Petrie's enormous photographic collection of over eight thousand excavation and object negatives also needed sorting and identification. In the early eighties it became necessary to copy the three thousand or so cellulose nitrate negatives, which constituted a potential fire hazard, onto modern safety film. This took four years to accomplish and was paid for by the museum's sales-profits, with the addition of grant-aid from the Area Museums Service for South Eastern England, a body which has assisted many worthwhile projects over the years. At present, the Department's collection of glass lantern slides is being reformatted onto 35mm. film. The negative archive itself is still in the course of being documented by a volunteer, who has already devoted twelve years to this task. It is consulted not only by Egyptologists, but also by avid photographers. We have even enjoyed a visit from the editors of the American based *Pinhole Journal*, Petrie having been a devotee of this particular type of camera.

On the 1st June 1988, the day that the collection re-opened to the public, the organization called the 'Friends of the Petrie Museum' (PMF) was launched to engage the interest and help of enthusiasts of Egyptology in the enjoyment and safeguarding of its antiquities. A full programme of lectures, museum seminars (Figure 27), and social activities is provided by the staff and associates of the Department and the voluntary committee. There have even been ambitious 'Petrie Expeditions' to view the aegyptiaca in Leiden and Berlin. A lively newsletter is produced, recently short-listed for an award. Over the last four years the Friends have greatly contributed to pressing conservation projects: the restoration of a flood-damaged Late Period coffin, and of some of the previously treated Hawara portraits, which had been damaged during the renovation. They are currently supporting the cleaning of the others. The world-wide membership now numbers four hundred, and is increasing steadily. Indeed, the Friends play a similar rôle as those who, a century ago, helped to fund the excavations which brought the material to the collection.

Modern museum work in the nineties is rather different from that undertaken by Arkell and Burgess almost forty years ago. The services provided have greatly increased over the decades, for as the museum has become more accessible, so the demands from both scholars and the general public have multiplied. Correspondence inquiries arrive daily

27. *Registering flints: a 'Museum Practice' seminar for the Friends, 1990. (Courtesy of Mr. L. Robinson-Smith.)*

parties from every kind of institution to be guided around the displays. In 1991 nearly fifteen hundred people visited the museum: an all-time record. Petrie would delight in seeing his legacy so actively used today. Through all these many activities, the basic and essential cataloguing must be doggedly continued. Forty thousand objects have now been recorded, almost three times as many as when Arkell retired in 1963.

A development of the utmost significance occurred in 1991 when full museum registration was obtained from the Museums and Galleries Commission. This implied that the collection had reached an acceptable professional level in the areas of curatorial expertise, funding, acquisition and disposal policy, conservation provision, publication, and public access and service. The recognized status is increasingly required by official grant-giving bodies and potential donors. Our registration certificate has pride of place in the foyer to the Department, especially as we had had to be content with only provisional registration for two years because a formal management committee for the museum did not exist. That was subsequently achieved by reconstituting the College Art Collections Committee and renaming it the College Collections Committee. Over the years, this body has ensured the continuance and increase of our triennial conservation grant.

In the absence of any budget for running the museum, a programme of self-help was engendered when, back in 1977, a small sales point was started. The first ventures were a small guidebook, which is constantly updated and re-issued, and packs of slides. Fifteen years later the range is much expanded, as shown by the sales list which runs into four pages. Recent enterprises take the form of a poster produced by the Friends, replicas, jewellery, and even ten thousand bioplastic carrier bags! The revenue generated, together with that from charges and fees, is put towards vital museum projects.

Our postcards are now selling very briskly, particularly since Egyptology is at present on

from all over the world; there are also photographic orders to be processed, and samples to be selected for programmes of scientific analysis.

The number of loans to British and foreign exhibitions has grown out of all proportion during the last ten years, requiring curatorial attention to the details of valuation, packing, transport, photography, and display. Among the more important loans are those to the pottery exhibition 'Umm el-Ga'ab', in Cambridge (1982); 'Elfenbein im Alten Aegypten', in Erbach and Hanover (1987), consisting almost exclusively of ivories from the Petrie Museum; 'Pharaohs and Mortals', in Cambridge and Liverpool (1988), to which, for the first time, went the famous Sesostris relief from Koptos (see pages 8 and 48); 'The First Egyptians', Prehistoric objects travelling through the United States (1988-90); 'Everyday Life in Ancient Egypt', travelling around the West Midlands (1990); and Neolithic and Predynastic objects and toys and games to two exhibitions in Marseilles (1990 and 1991). Finally, in our Centenary year some of our New Kingdom treasures, including the Ebony Negress (see Figure 25) who had already travelled to Boston for 'Egypt's Golden Age' (1982), are on loan to the Cleveland Museum of Art for a travelling exhibition 'Egypt's Dazzling Sun: Amenhotep III and His World'.

In addition to assisting individual visitors who come to work on specific items, there are the National Curriculum for seven to eight year olds, which promotes much interest in all the museum has to offer the younger generation (Figure 28). For this reason we recently added a new set of six postcards.

It is the museum attendant who is responsible for operating the sales point. A new era of efficiency in the smooth day-to-day running of the collection was heralded by Smith's success in persuading the Provost that we needed a permanent attendant employed by the Department, instead of being allocated one of the College beadles. Finances were found and in 1988 the existing beadle, Mr. Patrick Byrne, became the first holder. A year later his place was filled by Mr. Roy Galloway.

The last two decades have witnessed several other staff changes, beginning in 1974 when Miss Rosalind Hall (now Mrs. Janssen, the Assistant Curator) was appointed as Research Assistant, in succession to Miss Joyce Townend. When Miss Anthea Page resigned in 1981 to start her own publishing company, her place as Departmental Secretary was taken by Mrs. Elizabeth Keyzar (now Mrs. Blyth).

In 1978 Dr. Geoffrey Martin took over from Dr. David Dixon as Honorary Curator (later Honorary Director); the same year he was promoted to Reader in Egyptian Archaeology. Then, in June 1986, Harry Smith surrendered the Edwards Chair, although he retained his position as Head of Department for a further two years in order to see the refurbishment of the Petrie Museum through to completion. Now Professor Emeritus, he continues to teach as much as ever, albeit on a part-time basis. Martin first received a personal professorship in 1987. A year later, he succeeded to the Edwards Chair, as the first alumnus of the College ever to hold the post. His Inaugural Lecture, delivered on the 28th April 1988, and entitled: 'The People of Memphis in the time of Tutankhamun and his Successors', reflects his specialization.

In 1989 the teaching of Egyptology at the School of Oriental Studies at Durham ceased. That August its lecturer, Dr. W. John Tait, was transferred to UCL, where he now shares the language tuition with Smith. At the same time the University of Durham sent several hundred volumes to the Edwards Library. These works, which principally cover Egyptian philology, including Coptic, filled long-standing gaps in the holdings, and have proved invaluable for the newly-instituted courses and degrees. In

October 1990 Mr. David G. Jeffreys, a UCL graduate in Hebrew with Egyptian, was appointed Lecturer in Egyptian Archaeology.

Four years previously, Jeffreys had taken over from Smith as Director of the Memphis Project for the Egypt Exploration Society. He now excavates there during the first academic term, Martin directing the E. E. S.-Leiden expedition at Saqqara in the second, while Barbara Adams is involved in the American work at Hierakonpolis. So the tradition of intensive fieldwork intended by Miss Edwards and pursued by Petrie and Emery is fully maintained and even expanded.

28. *Matthew Coy, aged eight, following* The Petrie Museum Children's Trail, *November 1991. (Courtesy of Mr. L. Robinson-Smith.)*

Thus in 1992 the Department has reached its present all-time peak of seven academic and two administrative members of staff. For the future, both financial stringency at home and political circumstances abroad may conceivably threaten to restrict its work as envisaged by our foundress Miss Amelia Edwards. But the undaunted enthusiasm which has inspired us since the days of her first professor, Flinders Petrie, will, we trust, continue unabated as we now enter the second hundred years.

Selected Sources

A. UCL Records Office

Committee minutes, etc.

1. Council 1892-1906 (=) College Committee 1907-77 (=) Council 1978-92
2. Senate 1892-1908 (=) Professorial Board 1909-76 (=) Academic Board & Executive Committee 1977-92
3. Committee of Management 1892-1908 (=) Managing Sub-Committee 1909-52 (=) Managing Committee 1953-68
4. Faculty of Arts & Science 1892-96 (=) Faculty of Arts & Laws 1896-1915 (=) Arts 1916-66

Printed Sources

University College London Calendars	1892 - 1992
University College London Annual Reports	1892 - 1988
University College London Gazette	1895 - 1904
University College London Union Magazine	1904 - 1919
University College Magazine	1920 - 1938

Miscellaneous Sources

Trust Fund Boxes	1892, 1893, 1936
Guard Books (= Scrapbooks)	1919 - 1964
War Correspondence Boxes	1939 - 1946
War Photographs Folder	1940 - 1945
UCL Fellows Correspondence	

Record Office Files

6/-/-	Egyptology 1930-1946		6/3/21	Miss Amelia B. Edwards
6/1/1	V. C. Lafleur		6/3/26	Egyptology - General
6/1/2	A. J. Arkell		45/1/57	Miss J. Tudor-Pole
6/1/3	Prof. J. Černý		45/1/109	Miss D. V. W. Kirkbride
6/1/4	J. Mellaart		45/2/14	Miss N. Whitaker (1930-45 Appointments)
6/1/5	General Staffing File		116/209	Margaret Murray Prize
6/1/6	Chair of Egyptology (Černý & Emery)		136/23	150th Anniversary
6/1/7	Prof. W. B. Emery		139/10	College Collections
6/1/8	R. O. Faulkner		143/1/32	H. S. Smith Inaugural Lecture
6/1/9	Readership in Egyptology		143/1/142	G. T. Martin Inaugural Lecture
6/1/10	H. S. Smith		299/58	Griffith Fund
6/1/11	D. M. Dixon		299/145	Margaretta Kirby Bequest
6/1/12	Miss J. Townend		299/236	S. Glanville Prize Fund
6/1/13	Mrs. J. Samson		299/280	Flinders Petrie Fund
6/3/10	Egyptological Collections		299/354	Gertrude Caton-Thompson Bequest
6/3/16	Centenary of Flinders Petrie's Birth		303/4	Egyptology Accommodation
6/3/19	Dr. Margaret Murray		347/1	Friends of Petrie
6/3/20	Sir Flinders Petrie			

B. College Library Archives

Library Committee minutes, 1945.
Files on the Edwards Library; Sir Alan Gardiner; Dr. Violet MacDermot.

C. College Library - Manuscripts & Rare Books

Uncatalogued College Correspondence 1892 *sqq.*
Papers on the subscription fund for the purchase of Petrie's Egyptian collection 1913-14.
MS ADD 335: Speeches at the Petrie Centenary 1953.

Appendix 1
Departmental Staff
1892~1992

EDWARDS PROFESSORS

W. M. F. Petrie	1892 - 1933
S. R. K. Glanville	1935 - 1946
J. Černý	1946 - 1951
W. B. Emery	1951 - 1970
H. S. Smith	1970 - 1986
G. T. Martin	1988 -

SECRETARIAL STAFF

Florence Mackenzie	1936 - 1939
Nonie Whitaker	1945
Jean Carroll (Tudor-Pole)	1946 - 1953
Diana Kirkbride	1949
Cynthia Cox	1953 - 1967
Anthea Page	1967 - 1982
Elizabeth Blyth (Keyzar)	1982 -

PRE-WAR HONORARY MUSEUM STAFF

W. M. F. Petrie; Margaret Murray; Hilda Petrie;
S. R. K. Glanville; Elise Baumgärtel; Violette Lafleur

POST-WAR MUSEUM STAFF

Violette Lafleur	1939 - 1954
A. J. Arkell	1948 - 1963
Diana Kirkbride	1950 - 1952
E. M. Burgess	1953 - 1963
S. C. L. Harris	1963 - 1965
H. S. Smith	1963 - 1967
Barbara Adams (Bishop)	1965 -
Joyce Townend	1965 - 1974
D. M. Dixon	1967 - 1978
Rosalind Janssen (Hall)	1974 -
G. T. Martin	1978 - 1987

PRINCIPAL POST-WAR RESEARCH STAFF

Julia Samson (Lazarus)	1966 -
H. M. Stewart	1970 -

TEACHING STAFF

F. Ll. Griffith	1893 - 1901
W. E. Crum	?1893 - 1910
J. H. Walker	1893 - 1914
Margaret Murray	1899 - 1935
H. F. H. Thompson	1915 - 1916
Georgina Aitken	1919 - 1929
Miss Rutherford	1924
Edith Guest	1924 - 1933
Lorna Weber	1928 - 1929
S. R. K. Glanville	1933 - 1935
J. H. Plenderleith	1935
Elise Baumgärtel	1936 - 1941
I. E. S. Edwards	1936; 1950
Margaret Drower	1940 - 1941
A. J. Arkell	1948 - 1963
J. Mellaart	1950 - 1951
R. O. Faulkner	1954 - 1967
H. S. Smith	1963 -
D. M. Dixon	1967 -
G. T. Martin	1970 -
W. J. Tait	1989 -
D. G. Jeffreys	1990 -

ASSOCIATED CONSERVATORS

R. L. & Helena Jaeschke	1980 -

MUSEUM ATTENDANTS

P. Byrne	1985 - 1989
R. C. J. Galloway	1989 -

( ) Indicates the former surname, also referred to in the text.

W. M. F. Petrie 1892 - 1933

S. R. K. Glanville 1935 - 1946

J. Černý 1946 - 1951

W. B. Emery 1951 - 1970

H. S. Smith 1970 - 1986

G. T. Martin 1988 -

Appendix 2

Petrie's Introductory Lecture
14th January 1893

We are met today at a landmark in the organization of historical research, to join in the opening of the first public establishment in England for the study of Egyptology. In other countries there have long been those facilities for students which we have lacked here. Germany, France, and Italy have been far better provided than ourselves, owing largely to the wide-minded views of their governments, which have sent expeditions of research and published grand works. England, on the contrary, has occupied Egypt for ten years, without the smallest recognition by the government of its historical importance; and even private enterprise has been hindered rather than helped by English diplomacy.

The only public teaching on our subject that has been attempted, was in the classes for the languages of Egypt and Assyria, started many years ago in London; but no other branches beside language were dealt with, and that did not command sufficient interest for the experiment to be continued. In later years Egypt has appeared as one element of general archaeology; in such a wide field, however, but little detail can be considered.

Of the importance of the study of Egypt, I need say nothing here; for indeed, of all food for the mind none is more strengthening and vital than history. For training the sense of proportion, for exercising careful deduction, for quickening the perception of minute facts, for creating a power of work, the study of history is a grand agent.

One of the most valuable gains from these researches in the past is what may be called the 'historical sense': the realization that everything is in continual flow and change; that all we see must have had efficient causes, and will have proportionate effects; that no matter how strange or unreasonable a form or a custom may be, it must imply an adequate cause behind it.

By 'history' we do not mean merely a verbal record, such as some connect with that word. Every fragment of the products of the past is concrete history. Everything is a document to the archaeologist. The greatness and the cruelty of Rome is more powerfully told by the Colosseum than by any words; a Greek temple, a French fan, an Egyptian statue, are more eloquent than any description. We raise from the dust the body of material facts of history, and the written word gives life and speech to it.

As yet there have been no encouragements provided for the student of Egyptian history. It has not been possible to read the essential works without spending a small fortune in purchases, or wasting hours in waiting for the works in some great library. The only collections have been rigorously preserved from close handling, or are inaccessible in private houses. There has been no centre of information nor union for students at work. Hence there have been but few students, although the frequent enquiries made, from time to time, show how many would wish to know more on the subject.

At last the present provision for study has arisen, but at how great a cost we all know. We must indeed mourn as well as rejoice this day. For in the loss of Amelia Blanford Edwards, whose devotion to Egyptology thus survives her, all who knew her must indeed feel that they have lost a true-hearted friend; and those who but knew her labours will regret their untimely close. Her constant devotion to the subject has built up a general interest in it, both in this land and in America, which may, if cultivated, yield rich fruit in the future. Her work must be continued, so far as possible: she sowed the seed, here we hope to raise the plants. Her example should be followed and her wishes fulfilled by us. Her untiring energy, her practical views, her absence of prejudice, and constant openness to argument and conviction were rare qualities indeed - as well as her unfailing good-feeling and kindly nature, which made enmities impossible. Seldom, indeed, is an endowment accompanied by so rich a moral bequest to those who would follow.

While dwelling on our loss, another name must not be forgotten on this day - Greville John Chester, to whom our national museum is largely indebted. He was a warm friend of the foundress, one who laboured for years to preserve and to spread the knowledge of Egyptian antiquities, and he would have rejoiced to be with us this day. We hope to commemorate him, in the library, by a selection of books subscribed by his friends in his name.

We must now turn from the past to the present. Owing to the new building of this College not yet being finished, the proper arrangement of our materials must be delayed until the summer. I hope that then you will find here a library in which every useful work on Egyptian antiquities will be at hand; every work, that is to say, containing inscriptions and drawings, accounts by early travellers, and the labours of scholars on the history, language, religion and civilization of Egypt. There are the rival claims of two classes of readers to be reconciled. Those who need to refer to many volumes at once, and must have a complete library, and those who can only study in spare hours at home. I shall therefore make an attempt at uniting a reference and a lending library here; and if it is not quite so convenient to either class as they would wish it to be, I must ask their forbearance on the ground of its fulfilling other needs. The proposal is that, during the greater part of the first and third term in each year, the library shall be open for reference on three mornings in the week, and shall then be complete, maintaining this rule by unhesitating action against defaulting borrowers. While during the other half of these weeks, all the vacations, and the second term, the books may be lent out, against a sufficient security.

Beside the books there will be a collection of over a thousand photographs; and these are of the greatest importance in showing the gradations of Egyptian art and style, which are obscured or lost in almost any hand copying. To those who cannot study original monuments photographs are essential, in order to grasp the continual changes which took place, and to understand the appearance of the monuments.

This library will also be a long-needed home for those paper impressions, or 'squeezes', of sculptures, which are invaluable for study, but which are too readily thrown aside and lost, owing to their size and the care they require. A series of such impressions will be a great help to the student.

Beside these materials on paper there will also be a collection of original objects which can be closely examined by students. Miss Edwards had formed a collection with much care, aiming that it should be as complete and typical as possible in a small space, so as to serve for teaching purposes. I hope to place here on loan my own collection; and to have a series of annual loan exhibitions drawn from the many and valuable private collections in England. Thus the student will find here a collection of deities, the most complete collection of scarabs, the only chronological collection of beads; many tools, a dated series of pottery,

the largest collection of funerary cones; also of Egyptian weights, with many of other countries, together with a mass of materials on technical arts. For certain lines of study therefore this will not be merely supplementary to, but will be in advance of any national museum. Every object will be dated so far as is possible, and the sequence of forms will be treated as in the Pitt Rivers Collection at Oxford.

Passing now from materials to personal work, I hope to give a series of lectures in the autumn and spring of each session, with the aim of presenting results intelligibly to those who have no special acquaintance with the subject. Besides this I shall endeavour to help all who may be really studying, by attending in the library at those hours when it is open to readers, three mornings in the week. As one of the most urgent needs is to prepare students who may wish to undertake practical work in Egypt, I propose to work in Egypt - usually on excavations - during each winter term, from before Christmas until Easter, and I shall personally help in every way those who may wish to join me for that term. For those who cannot leave England, there will be provided in this interval weekly lessons in the language and the inscriptions, at the College. Thus I hope in this - as in the case of the library - to combine the requirements of different classes of students. If we are to induce students to take up that active work in Egypt which is so greatly needed, it will not do to require of them the rare combination of abilities, time, and money, all at once. If they can provide the ability and the time, it ought to be the care of others to help in the cost. I say this the more freely because almost any careful and judicious excavation in Egypt repays the actual outlay by the antiquities found. So in appealing to others to help, I am only asking them to make an investment on behalf of some museum. To be more definite, I may say that £300 or £400 will provide the costs of travelling, living, excavating, and transport of collections, for one excavator for a season. The experience of my own work has averaged about that for some years past. We could keep three or four excavators in full work on different sites, if we were to provide in England £1000 or £1200 a year, and we might have about two hundred cases of antiquities to distribute, after satisfying the Egyptian Government. These are not speculative figures, they are simply the average results of my own work.

I see no difficulty in our raising such a sum, knowing what great interest there is in the matter; and if this is practically taken up I shall be glad to propose a treasurer for this trust. The arrangements of it I should keep in hand, subject to consulting any special wishes of those who contributed; while it would be quite clear of my own excavations, which will continue on the same footing as before with private friends. I hope to see this Egyptian Research Account fill a large part in the development of Egyptology in England.

Now we will pass from our means to our ends in view. Egyptology has been too often taken as a name for the study of the language alone. It is far more than that; it is the whole history of a great civilization. When we look at the priceless volume *Die Aegyptologie* by the greatest authority of all - Brugsch Pasha - we see how wide a field it covers; although naturally it is treated largely from his special side, by one who is a giant in the study of the language. It is the whole history and geography of Egypt that we have to deal with. If we open a good history book of our own land we find in it six different kinds of history all represented; and it is so easy to lose sight of any one of them, while pursuing the others, that it is well to put them separately before us. There is first the dynastic history, the lists of kings, dates, and royal events. Second, the political history of constitutions, of laws, and of wars. Third, the personal history of characters, the most potent, the most fascinating, the most informing of all. Fourth, the spiritual history of faiths, ideals, and views of life. Fifth, the aesthetic history of art, of architecture, sculpture, painting, and literature. Sixth, the material history of civilization in the necessaries of life, in science, in manufactures. Of all these only the dynastic, political, and spiritual, have ever been worked out in Egypt; and great spaces yet remain untouched. The personal, the artistic, and the material have scarcely been looked at.

In political history we have the main works of Brugsch and Wiedemann - the one without a reference or detail in it, the other a compendium of references - while, later than these is the more general history of Meyer. There are also compilations, such as *The Egypt of the Past*, in which Miss Edwards had a large share, and the later works of Rawlinson; but all these need large revision at present.

In religious history there are the publications of the Musée Guimet. In law Revillout has published most, but on the documents of late times.

The general outlines of the attainments of the Egyptians in art and material life were laid down, with remarkable fullness for the time, by Wilkinson, in a work which all have borrowed from, and none have rivalled. Yet, that is not a history; there is scarcely any tracing of historical development, nor appreciation of the continual changes which occurred, and little stress is laid on the most obvious differences of the periods.

In considering what direction our work here should best follow, we may well take the words of Professor Schuster at the last meeting of the British Association. He said: 'I should like to see it more generally recognized that although there is no struggle for existence between different nations, yet each nation owing to a number of circumstances possesses its own peculiarities, which render it better fitted than its neighbours to do some particular part of the work on which the progress of science depends.' He then proceeded to instance the genius of France for accurate measurement, of Germany for logical development and testing of theories, of England for mathematical physics.

Applying these wide views to our present case, we may say that the study of the religion and law of Egypt is particularly the taste of the French, the language has its greatest exponents in Germany. For ourselves - the only classical work of England is that of Wilkinson, on the artistic and material civilization. To this side we may then well devote our attention, without rejecting any other part to which discoveries may draw us.

Not only is systematic study needed in all points of the regions I have mentioned, but in each line a general collection is required of all the materials available in various museums. And this need of a *corpus* of drawings and descriptions for each class of objects, is felt by foreign scholars as well, who will gladly welcome such an advance.

I will now indicate some of the subjects which will, I hope, be taken up here, either by myself, or by others who may be drawn to make this a centre of work.

The art of Egypt needs much more systematic study than it has yet received. Not only should the details of the various periods be clearly separated, but also the various schools or local centres of art, the products of any one of which have a strong likeness throughout varying ages. To treat art as if it varied only with age, and not with place, would be like confounding together all paintings of the fifteenth century, and then making another group of those of the sixteenth, regardless of whether Flemish or French, Venetian or Umbrian. To clear up these local schools, the material must be our main guide. Any one who has studied the statuary knows at a glance the differing characteristics of the limestone school, the quartzite school, the red granite school, the black granite school, or the basalt school. The situation of these schools needs to be fixed by local explorations in search of the stone and the quarries. The architecture has still need of much detailed work, to determine the rules of each period; and also of research into the earlier ages, where its prehistoric forms may be seen fossilized in the hieroglyphs depicting the various forms then used. The translation of Egyptian forms to other lands, Syria and Greece, also needs historical examination.

The geography has been much clarified, of late years, by exploration but many points are yet undecided, and there is room for work in the study as well as in the field.

The principles of name-giving and the history of personal names in Egypt is an entirely untouched subject. The merely childish names, the good-wish names, the dedicatory names, those derived from peculiarities, and many other classes, require unravelling, sorting and reducing to historical statistics. The titles of office have been treated, by Brugsch, in his *Wörterbuch* and his work *Die Aegyptologie*. But what needs now to be compiled is a directory of all Egyptian officials, under their titles. This could show the historical rise and decay of the offices, their relative importance, and much of their nature; and often serve to identify monuments belonging to one person. Much of this directory is already compiled, so I hope no-one will hastily begin to go over the ground again.

The history of hieroglyphs is a subject still to let. We require to know the original object intended by each form, the reason for selecting that object for the idea, and the changes which the form has undergone in all ages, and the amount of variation in each period. Here is work for some lives and it is to be hoped that any one taking it up will well consider the plan of work, and so labour that others may add to his results without needing to repeat them.

The presence of foreign races in Egypt, from all points of the compass still needs much exploration, to explain what little we know. Much has come to light in recent years: but only enough to tantalize us. Certainly, it is of the first importance for the history of the world to trace the influences and relations of Egypt. Her continuous history and the constant use of royal names make her links the only clues to tracking the prehistoric darkness of other lands. The chronology of Egypt becomes then of world-wide importance. Greatly as estimates about it have varied in past years, we at least know now that it cannot have varied beyond tolerably definite limits. The idle position of those who would ignore chronology, because it is not exact, can no longer be justified; and from continuous astronomical statements we are warranted in believing that as far back as the sixteenth century B.C. we are on solid ground; and even the beginning of monumental history is probably known within two or three centuries. I hope that here we may extend and consolidate the fixed data of history.

On more practical lines there is much need of trained hands for excavation and exploration, and any one with time and health will do well to turn to this cause. No greater mistake is made than supposing that an excavator must needs be a scholar. Totally different qualities are needed by the two. To take a parallel, the Astronomer Royal may publish the Nautical Almanac, and be responsible for its intricate accuracy, but he is not therefore fitted to navigate an ironclad. The navigator needs to know not merely how to use the almanac, but needs also a great many practical qualities, which the astronomer has not. The excavator needs many qualities which are quite outside the province of the scholar, but he does not need all the scholar's knowledge of the language and history. For either to take up the other's work, would produce as unhappy a result as for the astronomer and the navigator to exchange their functions. In connection with this, the work of archaeological surveying is one that is much needed. Different methods and different eyes are required from those of an ordinary land-surveyor, and it is to be hoped that some may follow up this line.

We turn now to the subjects which each require a *corpus* of materials to be gathered and systematically reduced to historical order.

Of the pottery we have - from the work of recent years - an almost complete series through the whole of Egyptian history. Most of the types have been published in various works, but it is still desirable to unite all the information in one handbook of Egyptian pottery, expressing the forms, colours and materials. The pottery is not of particular value, nor of much beauty, in general; but it is essential for a key to the age of other objects, as it is universally spread on all sites.

The funerary figures or ushabtis have been occasionally published, but no comparative series of them is arranged, to show their historical changes. We need a systematic catalogue of all the ushabtis known; such a *corpus* would throw great light on them.

The scarabs with personal names of kings and officials have been partially published, and I am hoping to issue an enlarged edition of the *corpus* when more material is available. Already good historical results have come from this collection: for instance, the determination of the name Khian [Khyan] for the king whose statue was found at Bubastis, and the fixing of his epoch to the Xth dynasty [this should be the XVth dynasty], where his name occurs in the Karnak list of kings.

The history of beads is not merely a fascinating triviality, but as they are the most widespread objects - next to pottery - their exact dating is of historical value. Especially is this the case when they are found as exported objects in foreign countries. It is by a peculiar type of bead that we can give an approximate date to the later tombs at Mycenae. You will find in this collection the only dated series of beads that has yet been formed. I hope that when that is more complete, an illustrated *corpus* will be published as a guide to historical research.

Glass and the earlier manufacture of glaze much need elucidation. The colours of glaze are now pretty well known historically, mainly from scarabs, rings, and dated vases. And now that we have a large series of glass colours, and designs of patterned glass vases, dated to Khuenaten [Akhenaten], 1400 B.C., there is a firm footing for beginning the study of glass. A good colourist is most needed to take up the formation of a *corpus* of glass and glazes. Fortunately Mr. Henry Wallis has done much in the latter branch, and is now drawing all the glazed vases in the Giza Museum. Other workers, even though of less artistic skill, are much needed; and they must not merely make pretty sketches, but rigorously accurate, hand-drawn, copies.

The subject of metallurgy and chemistry has only been touched by a dozen or twenty analyses. There is need of a much greater amount of research here; but dated specimens of alloys and compounds are required, and these cannot be usually obtained except from scientific excavations. Dr. Gladstone has given us some very interesting results, of late; and we now know that a long age of copper preceded the use of bronze in Egypt.

The history of the forms of tools and weapons has not yet been attempted. We know now the types of knives and chisels of the XIIth and XVIIIth dynasties, but very little else. Here again scientific excavation is necessary for dated examples. Perhaps these may be treated best in connection with the development of tools in other lands, which is an even darker subject than it is in Egypt.

The types of coffins, both of stone and wood are as yet unclassified; and no-one can accurately state when any particular form or decoration came into use or disappeared. A complete *corpus* of drawings or photographs of all dated coffins in museums is required to settle the subject; and this would fix the age of the far larger number of undated examples, and so be of much value.

Of amulets we know very little. The types are familiar, but scarcely anything is known of their order, or position on the mummies, except in a few instances which I have found. We need to ascertain their variations of form, when they arose and disappeared, what position each usually occupied, and what ideas were connected with each. Unfortunately again, very little can be done without scientific - and lucky - excavation.

Toilet objects, such as mirrors, kohl vases and spoons, are familiar enough; but yet we remain in ignorance of what modifications they underwent; and no-one can, as yet, tell the date of a mirror from its form. Much may here be done by drawing and photographing in museums, especially on any inscribed specimens. A complete list of all peculiar examples is needed.

Jewellery is very rare, whether dated or undated. But such an attractive subject should not long wait for an historian. Of the later types of Roman age, the portraits of ladies painted in coloured wax and the relief modelled stucco cases give us valuable dated indications.

On weights and measures there is still ample room for work. It is true, we can now reckon our specimens by the thousand, instead of by the dozen as we did a few years ago. But fresh and intricate problems arise as materials increase; and yet again accurate excavation is almost the only key to this subject, as to so many others.

I have now briefly noticed some of the various subjects of interest that await our time, our patience, and our analysis. Surely some of those whose tastes lie in this direction will not remain in the camp of the dilettanti. Resolute and accurate work, well finished, is what we need, on however small a scale. Someone may not be able to touch more than a minute subject, in a few spare hours, now and then; but yet let him do that fully and completely, and every student will thank him.

My ultimate hope is to see drawn together here, a solid body of workers, each contributing some permanent advance to our knowledge. I do not mean by this in the least that only those who can give a large amount of time can be of use. Much of our best scientific work is done in the stray hours of busy men. It is the glory of England that - if a nation of shopkeepers - they are such shopkeepers as can equal the scientific specialists of other lands. We do not depend on officials, nor men who make a profession of their science, for all our work. We see around in every direction the free worker rivalling the specialist. Murchison, Spottiswoode, Huggins, De La Rue, Evans, Lubbock - these are household names; and yet all their work was done outside of the course of life which most men would consider full enough without a scientific reputation. Can we not expect to see arise a Murchison or an Evans of Egyptology?

Here I hope to meet with all those who will and can work; to help their start in one direction or another, so far as I can; to join with them in excavations in Egypt, and see thus a school of scientific excavation arise, to clear away the darkness in which we now stumble.

Here the means of study and research will be provided so far as possible. The future lies with you.

Index

Page numbers in italic refer to illustrations